THE MOM IN ME

Stories and Practical Advice from Moms Who have Survived Parenting

VISIONARY AUTHOR
KIMMOLY K. LABOO

ISBN-13: 978-1-7351126-6-4
Library of Congress Control Number: 2020918964

For information regarding special discounts for bulk purchases contact the Publisher:
LaBoo Publishing Enterprise, LLC
staff@laboopublishing.com
www.laboopublishing.com

All information is solely considered as the point of view of the authors.

TABLE OF CONTENTS

INTRODUCTION

Being a mom is the one job women try desperately to do exceptionally well. From the moment we find out we are pregnant we set out to make sure everything is perfect for the child we are carrying and eventually plan to give birth to. We take our prenatal vitamins, attend doctor's appointments, shop for clothes, buy the best cribs, strollers, breast pumps, onesies, and binkies. However, no matter how hard we try to be the perfect mom, nothing can really prepare us for this thing called motherhood. The journey is full of twists and turns, joy, tears, and fear, but we wouldn't trade it for anything else in this world.

I've heard it said that being a mom is like watching your heart walk around outside of your body. No matter how protective we are there are some things guaranteed to be out of our control. Yet, as mothers, we put on our brave faces and we set out to conquer and overcome whatever challenges motherhood throws our way.

Twenty-one valiant moms have collaborated to share how they have pushed through and survived seemingly insurmountable obstacles. Being a mom isn't about being perfect. I promise you, there is no perfect mom on this earth. What you will see in the pages of this book is the strength, determination, and courage of these incredible moms, told through the experiences they have endured along one of the most daring journeys we as women can ever attempt - motherhood.

There are many books that will tell you what to do when you are expecting a child. Yet few tackle what it is like to go through the growing stages and many struggles that children may face and how to support them. In these pages you will find some advice, lots of encouragement, and what may feel like a gigantic hug from moms who want you to know that you are doing just fine!

Give yourself a break…you've got this!!!

"A mother's arms
are more comforting
than anyone else's."

— **Princess Diana**

Cheryl A.S. Hurley is an extraordinary woman who embraces her life's mission wholeheartedly. A certified Life Coach with a passion for tapping potential and maximizing prospects, she is an expert with over 20 years' experience in creating an open and safe space for individuals to clarify intentions, expand possibilities and reach new heights.

Cheryl coaches' women to conquer their fears, achieve their dreams and realize their unique purpose despite the circumstances they may have faced. Born in Philadelphia, Pennsylvania, Cheryl A.S. Hurley has always been a positive influence on her family, friends, and colleagues.

Cheryl is married to Reginald S. Hurley, Sr., has two beautiful children (Reginald Jr. and Shannon) and four adorable grands – Jayden, Trinity, Reginald III and Ryan.

Her Motto: "The legacy that a woman leaves is the one she lives, walks and breathes."

STRENGTHENED BY THE STRUGGLE: PARENTING A CHILD WITH DEPRESSION

CHERYL A.S. HURLEY

To say this was an easy chapter to write would be untruthful. First and foremost, I was challenged by God to revisit some painful memories that brought forth tears, but in the end, were necessary to help and empower moms with practical tips and action steps to effectively and proactively support their children. It is my prayer and hope that you take the time to hear my heart as I share some painful experiences that I encountered due to missed signals. It is God's desire to shed light on childhood depression and its impact on families, particularly moms.

When the pronouncement comes that they are expecting, many moms are excited and carry their unborn child with anticipation for the arrival of a healthy bundle of joy. For those who get prenatal care, typically an amniocentesis test is performed around the five-month term of a pregnancy. This medical term denotes the test that obstetricians perform to remove fluid from the uterus of a pregnant woman for testing to detect any abnormalities of the unborn child. Once the results come back negative, it tends to alleviate all worry of any possible birth defects of the unborn child, and moms remain filled with excitement.

Precious... adorable... kissable...gentle...needy...

All of these are the magnificent emotions I experienced at the birth and nurturing of my precious little girl. The warm-colored outfits, the gentle blankets to keep her warm, the feedings, the bathing, the caring, and the mothering. Oh, how precious and wonderful to care for such a blessed bundle of joy.

Those toddler years were trying but I said to myself, "I can do this!" I can sit back now and laugh as I recall one Sunday morning getting ready for church. I had dressed my precious three-year-old in a gorgeous pink and white lacy dress with a beautiful pink satin sash with a big bow on it. I had these adorable custom-made socks with white ruffled lace stitching that nicely complemented her shiny white patent-leather shoes and her neatly styled ponytail with a beautiful pink bow. After looking at how adorable she was, I instructed her to sit down and quietly watch one of her favorite shows while Mommy got dressed. I ran upstairs and quickly finished getting dressed. When I finished grooming myself and was ready to go, I came downstairs and was in absolute shock. This little girl had ripped the bow off her dress, had a visible blue ink-pen line going down the front of her dress, the shiny white shoes were streaked with black scuff marks, and there was no evidence that she ever had a ponytail, let alone a bow in her hair! I was frustrated as 'I' had meticulously shopped for this outfit. I had gotten her dressed and look at what happened to 'my' creation! Ruined, I thought and shifted into what we moms call the 'fix-it' mode. Whew, I survived!

Then there was the early school-age stage when I often received comments from family and observers concerning how well-mannered and obedient my daughter was. *Yeah, I got this* (so I thought...). As I recall, there were moments where I found my daughter notably quiet, but I never gave much attention to it.

During the middle school years, my daughter attended a private school affiliated with the community development center where I served as an administrator. I recall receiving phone calls about my daughter showing increased aggression and fighting. In my head, I was like, *Where is this coming from? This chick was obedient, and suddenly, she's fighting?*

In my mind, I thought about how my husband and I were providing all the things parents strive to do such as food, shelter, clothing, good education, vacations, but something just didn't seem right. Nevertheless, I carried on and became more attentive, as I was beginning to become somewhat concerned.

The high school years were a whirlwind of highs and lows that were unexplainable. I felt as if I were in a full-fledged war. This beautiful young lady and I were in constant battle. I recall thinking, *I love her but I can't stand her!* 'I thought' she was irritable, disrespectful, and 'intentionally' violated 'my' authority.

I decreed that I wasn't having it!

The story that I told myself that *I can do this* was slowly fading away as I began to feel the hard stuff that constantly gnawed at my insides. I recall the midnight moments where I silently cried out to God, *If you don't do something I am going to break!* Moms, I was in pain, I was hurting, I had lost my zest for life and the things I desired to do. "What's the use?" I cried. And whether you can envision this or not, guess who was the recipient of my frustration and anger? It was my wonderful husband. It was so unfair, but he got it – the isolation, the accusations of teaming with my daughter, resulting in my, at times, rejecting him.

I believed God heard my prayers and finally gave me an instruction. *Cheryl, if you are going to parent this child, I need you to trust my divine guidance, relinquish 'your' anger, and humble yourself to be coached on how to handle this beautiful child I called STORM.*

The next several years became the educational years for the Mom in Me. This journey began with my willingness to learn how to put my racket down, take on one day at a time, give her space, focus on her giftedness, talents, and skills, and help her develop her character. I needed to let her be her and encourage her to allow me to be me.

We can now talk to each other and respect each other and allow time to be close and time to be apart. I had to recognize how I played a part in her aggression and anger by imposing my expectations upon her vs. allowing her to pace herself.

Was this easy? NO!!! But was it worth it? ABSOLUTELY!!! Not only did I learn about my daughter and me, I learned something to bless other mothers, regain my peace, and get my focus back! YES – it was most definitely worth it. I often tell mothers today, listen to your children and allow the Holy Spirit to equip you as you are led to be the healthy support they need.

The Education of the Mom in Me

I am a firm believer of where there is no truthfulness there can be no healing. It was in her late teens as she transitioned to young adulthood that I began to notice the mood swings my daughter had and my reaction to them.

I discovered that she struggled with depression. That was a huge wakeup call for me—and I beat myself up terribly! Here I was pointing the finger and trying to understand why at times I felt she was being difficult, when in actuality she was trying to cope with a challenge that she had no control over. How did I miss this? Here I was placing expectations upon her that at times were overwhelming. When I tell you she is a brain, that is an understatement.

I thought, *she is highly educated, intelligent, and has it going on.* Why did it take her days to complete her chores, the forgetfulness at times, the overwhelming restlessness, why she sometimes slept the day away or why she wanted to be close and at other times, seemingly didn't want to be bothered?

As I replayed those childhood moments, it all started to come together and make sense. As moms, it is important to recognize that each child has his or her personality and responds to experiences differently. They too, like us, may have outgoing, shy, balanced, or mild to challenging personalities. Yet it is vitally important to be in tune with your child's temperament, which allows you to treat them in a positive and caring manner that complements their personality. Make no mistake that this is crucial to nurturing their healthy emotional growth. Through understanding your child's personality, you can help them succeed by providing them with practical action steps and discipline that best fits their needs.

As our children grow, we may find ourselves searching for clues to their behavior. As moms, it is not uncommon to hear the words "developmental stages." This is just another way of saying they are moving through a certain period in the growing-up process. At times, they may be fascinated with their hands, feet, and mouth. As they grow, they will get into everything. Lock your doors, move your keys, and take a deep breath! Then there will be an age when independence is all they want. What's important is that at every stage, what they need is our love, our understanding, and our time.

The Face of Childhood Depression

When developmental delays or other concerns show up in our children, we obtain assessments, evaluations, and take action to get needed support as appropriate and necessary. But what do we do about children who have no prominent symptoms or are incorrectly labeled as troublemakers, or when we as moms unintentionally dismiss signals? This can often occur as a result of not understanding the face of depression.

It is normal for a child to occasionally feel sad or experience hopelessness, which is a part of every single child's life. However, a signal that some moms may miss is the almost invisible shift from happiness to feeling sad or uninterested in things that they used to enjoy, or they feel helpless or hopeless in situations they are unable to change. When this is persistent, it can be a sign of depression. Because a child often doesn't understand how to express what they are feeling, they may not talk about feelings of sadness, a lack of motivation or thoughts of helplessness. The Mom in Me did not see sadness.

However, through my gaining understanding about depression and its impact on our children, here are a few behaviors that I do recall seeing at some point:

- Sadness, hopelessness, and irritability
- Increased eating at times
- Irregular sleep patterns
- Overly stimulated or extremely tired
- A hard time paying attention
- Feeling worthless

Children with depression often have low self-esteem, negative social skills, lack contentment, are excessively self-critical, and often feel helpless when dealing with negative events. Depression may also be a response to verbal abuse, problems our kids experience at school, bullying, or peer pressure.

Identifying Childhood Depression

As I shared some of my experiences, I silenced the lie when I took my power back and began to educate myself about depression in children. Often, we may interpret a child's non-compliance to our expectations without recognizing there may be some underlying factors that make it difficult to impossible. As I did my research, I discovered some interesting characteristics among children with depression. So what is a child with depression like? If you were to ask them, they would say something like:

"I am loving, affectionate, and sympathetic to others. I feel sorry or sad when others are upset. I may even, if I choose, like to please you. I don't always need you close for protection because I like my independence, but please don't go too far away. I may, and most times will, do the exact opposite of what you desire. I may be uncompromising, not willing to wait, or give in. I may even be bossy, which I like. One of my favorite words is 'me.' Oh, and I may have fears of sounds, disengagement, rearranging household objects, or pets."

I want you to take a deep breath and pause. These are the loving characteristics of what a child with depression is like. A child with depression, may struggle with complying with our expectations. When that occurs, they would like you to know what they need is to feel loved and supported.

"I need to be able to travel down the block and go on outings to satisfy my curious side. I love my routines so please don't change them abruptly. I need you to notice not what I didn't do, but what I do well, and PRAISE me. I need you to give me two positive redirections to help me get back on track when I say 'no.' While I need my space, I need you to be in control and make decisions when I am unable to do so. I need you to be firm yet calm with me when I forget something or disagree with you. And no matter what, I need you to know that even though I may not act like it, I am doing my best to follow the expectations."

Having a transparent moment, I cried as I thought of the many situations where I misinterpreted my daughter's behavior as being difficult, as I never imagined that she was battling childhood depression. If you are like me, I didn't associate depression with some of the presenting behaviors I experienced. When I remembered those moments, I cried some more. There were moments where I battled with the feeling that I was a terrible mom.

I recall her sharing being bullied in middle and high school, which caused her to lash out, resulting in the perceived aggression. While in high school, she encountered a staff person who she had a great conflict with. My husband and I consulted with this staff person on several occasions in her defense, as she was infuriated to no end.

As I replayed the conversations we had with the staff person and her, it was clear to me what the challenge was. Rather than communicate with her from a place of calm when she disagreed and could hold her own (the child should be a lawyer as her gift of articulation is phenomenal), the staff person would yell and become aggressive, which became a trigger for her vs. the patience and understanding she needed.

Tips the Mom in Me Learned About Supporting a Child with Depression

One of the greatest trip-ups for me was learning how to start a conversation by knowing what to say and how to say it. It wasn't until I put my racket down that I was able to acknowledge how I contributed to my daughter's feelings of depression.

Here are a couple of tips I learned:

- Show my love by just being present. I'm a talker and often she didn't want to talk and just needed someone who understood what she was feeling.
- Schedule time for just the two of us to do something outside of the house, even if she didn't want to talk.
- Maintain normalcy and stick to a routine.
- Affirm her for positives and monitor the negatives.
- Be aware of my temperament to maintain calmness for healthier conversations.
- Be intentional to take care of me.

Grace for the Mom in Me for Other Moms

While it is the 21st century, and there is much research on depression, it is still very much an isolating illness. Even with the progress that has been made in knowledge, reducing the associated stigma, and treatment options, it is not uncommon for someone struggling with depression— or that person's family and friends—to feel alone. The Mom in Me wants to encourage you to break through the barriers associated with childhood depression. We must be the light for our children as they navigate through their depression by first taking time to self-care.

Self-care is critical for moms raising children with depression. As moms, yes, we love our children, but we must remember to make sure our needs are also being met. Even though time may be limited, take heed to that voice whispering in your head, reminding you that that lovely gift from God is counting on you. Here are several self-care tips for moms. Enjoy!!!

1. Mom in Me Self-Care Tip#1 – Get plenty of REST. Your sleep matters!
2. Mom in Me Self-Care Tip#2 – Maintain a healthy diet.
3. Mom in Me Self-Care Tip#3 – Exercise to manage stress.
4. Mom in Me Self-Care Tip#4 - Seek Help – Professional Help when necessary or otherwise when needed.
5. Mom in Me Self-Care Tip#5 - Be Bold – Be Courageous – Ask For Help!

Every mom will agree without reservation that parenting is a difficult job, but to parent a child with depression can be an exhausting, emotional experience. So how do we effectively achieve this? We seek forgiveness for what we do not know; we take time to care for ourselves; we take meaningful moments to practice mindfulness; and we love our children by understanding who they are and being what they need us to be – at the moment.

In closing, the Mom in Me prays that you remain encouraged and never give up. The journey to parenting a child with depression, depending upon the severity, can be overwhelming. However, a willingness to trust God for direction, to see your child beyond their behavior, to nurture them, to remain knowledgeable and informed of best practices, and to maintain your emotional well-being and self-care will empower the Mom in You to rise in Victory!

Even on days when you feel like you are failing, look around and I promise you, your kids will think you are the best mom in the WHOLE universe!

Cheryl A.S. Hurley

"Mothers hold their children's hands for a short while, but their hearts forever."

– Unknown

Andrea Riley is a young, single mother of three, on a mission to share her journey in life with others, letting them know how God brought her through various trials in life and that they are not alone. She serves in several public sector capacities including Deputy Director within the Mississippi Department of Mental Health. She is also Mental Health Certified. Andrea oversees the day to day operation for people with Intellectual and Developmental disabilities in their community programs. She has served her country for fifteen years with the MS Air National Guard and is an Operation Enduring Freedom Veteran.

Ms. Riley has worked with several nonprofit organizations both locally and nationally. She holds a Bachelor Degree in Public Health, a Master Degree in Public Administration with a Human Resources concentration, and an Organizational Management certification. She also holds a Doctoral Education Specialist degree in Adult Education. Ms. Riley has shared many aspects of her journey speaking at conferences and trainings.

MOMMY IS DEPRESSED

ANDREA J. RILEY

We admire the way a caterpillar transforms in the cocoon. We are amazed at the beautiful butterfly as it emerges after the process in such a wrapped space, rendering it immovable as it transforms.

Severe Chronic Depression is much like the process of a caterpillar, cocoon, and the beautiful butterfly, rendering a person immovable, unable to function in most day-to-day capacities in their life. It can be smothering, gripping and outright uncomfortable. When a mother is in a depressed state, we want so badly to play with our kids, to be happy with them, to find joy simply in seeing their face, but the state we are in during that time can be crippling. It is a dark and lonely place to be. However, if we can just remember while wrapped in the cocoon of depression, the beauty preparing to emerge, it will be free flying and just unimaginably happy again. This outlook helps to see some light peeking through the darkest of days. Make no mistake, depression didn't start for me after I had children. I suffered with depression as a teenager. I attempted suicide several times.

Usually when people meet me and get to know me, they are overcome with joy or happiness as they see a young, successful, level-headed woman. Many times, in conversations involving life or sharing my testimony, I ask the question, "When you look at me what do you see? Do you see a young lady who was molested several times as a child by multiple people? Do you see a broken, depressed, angry teenager who had all the support around her but had no idea how to reach out? Do you see a young adult who joined the military early in life, started a family early in life, and acquired multiple degrees and a fulfilling civilian career doing what she loves but was a single parent, broken, angry, depressed as well as stuck emotionally and psychologically? Do you see a young woman, who like Elijah, was literally begging God to take her life?" My journey from 2014 through 2019 was one which still amazes me how God brought me out.

Most people see a successful young lady who hit wonderful milestones early in life. They see a young lady who has worked hard and pushed herself, a great single mother who has clawed her way to beating many odds. They see a compassionate, caring, and intelligent woman. However, what they saw I didn't recognize. I functioned as her, yet I couldn't see her. I didn't know she existed.

Nothing was ever enough for me to me, so I worked to do more, be more, to validate the depression within me constantly telling me I was not good enough. I was never going to amount to anything. I fed the depression by piling my plate up with titles, degrees, and accomplishments. I also literally fed my depression by overeating, which eventually led me to be severely obese and facing several health problems by thirty. None of it satisfied the depression. In conjunction with the depression, the obesity and keeping myself engulfed in trying to accomplish more and more for validation to myself suffocated my ability to be a parent for much of my children's early childhood.

Each time I felt the weight begin to lift, another blow seemed to knock me right back to that dark place. It was familiar, comfortable. I was accustomed to what it felt like and became ok with it. In 2017, my youngest son was diagnosed with several issues after several rounds of testing, but the one delivering the hardest blow was Autism. It almost sent me in to a severe downward spiral, to say the least. As a statewide Autism Trainer, and a leader in the local mental health community, this was the hardest battle I faced with my children thus far.

Depression is a monster all on its own. Depression as a parent can have a person so far down, they see no way out. I know as a parent, I thought looking in my children's faces would make me happy. Why didn't it bring me a sense of joy? In a severe depression, it didn't seem to faze me. In my mind, being a parent in that place was more harm than good, so it was very difficult in a space of depression to be a mother. There were days I didn't want to be a mother. I felt I wasn't able to be a mother. To have children to parent in the mix of the daily life stressors can heighten the condition. It put me in a place between 'I have to do better for them' and 'it's not worth it.' A few years ago, I was in the 'it's not worth it' mindset. I was so bogged down and tired during the time. I was what some people would call a public success but a complete private mess. As a parent, I could not function at home. I spent hours in the bed. It was my best friend. All I wanted to do was sleep. I did not try to go out and be amongst people. I didn't really want people around me nor my children. The hardest part about it was, I could not figure out why. I didn't know why I felt the way I felt. There were times when I felt like I was going crazy. At one point the urge to commit suicide and take my kids with me was so strong, it was all I thought about at home. I could not figure out what was wrong with me.

Outside of my home, I was this successful woman who had accomplished all these milestones early in my life. People didn't see me in the bed crying myself to sleep. People didn't see me coming home and not helping with homework and not cooking. The world did not see me just not caring. If it was not going to affect us outside of our home, it didn't matter to me. If it did not have someone else's eyes on it, then I really didn't have much interest in it. My kids suffered. It was tough for me to be in such a place and be so immovable, unable to move myself from this somber place. I was so angry with my children and I am sure they had no idea why. It was not them; it was nothing they did. The effects it had on my children probably have been the hardest for me to deal with after coming out of such a dark place. They feared saying anything to me because I would be so tense at the sheer thought of a conversation with them. I was never physically abusive. I can now admit I was, in a sense, unintentionally, psychologically abusive.

Who wants to come home with a parent who takes a bath and gets in the bed? A parent who has no interest in what kind of day they had. I asked what they wanted to eat. I made sure they were fed, clothed, and cared for. However, I missed making sure they felt loved, protected, and guided. I was not parenting my kids. I was just there as the adult in the house. I made sure they had what they needed but put forth no effort to help them in any way. I mean I did the bare minimum as a parent in our house. If I had to help with homework, I would be in such a hurry to come in there to rush them through whatever so I could get in the bed. My bed became a place of solace. It was the one place I could shut the world entirely out. I was so busy. I was constantly moving outside the home, yet inside our home I was of no service to my children.

There came a time in 2018 when I could feel the fresh air and sun shining on my face. I noticed how my disposition and the way I talked to them affected their moods as well. Honestly, one of the most important actions I learned to do, coming out of what I call "the dark place," was to communicate with my children. To be able to say, "Hey I'm tired; just give me a minute alone." Moreover, those times when I am tired and frustrated require my ability to communicate such to them. Regardless of how we try to hide it, our children know when we are in a dark place more specifically by how we respond to them. Depression as a parent and as a single parent can be an even bigger monster than anything else we can face as parents. The singleness for me made it even worse, but not because I felt I needed a man. It was because I felt I had no one to vent to, no one to say, "It is okay not to be ok," no support system to help hold me up and pull me through in the flesh form.

I'm so grateful I never fed toxic things to my children about their fathers. This one area has always been vitally important to me, to keep their perceptions of their fathers innocent and allow them to form their own perspectives as they aged. It was always very important to me despite my own misery. I refused to paint their fathers in a negative light. I was always concerned with the damage it would cause and I did not want to be responsible for sowing those fruitless seeds into my children concerning their fathers. My mother did not do this either. I am eternally grateful in my life as a single parent that God gave me enough wisdom for those two specific areas.

The hardest part about dealing with severe and chronic depression is it doesn't go away, and it is relentless in its pursuit. Learning to manage depression as a parent is an important step in being able to effectively parent. Literally, it was miserable, and it was depressing in itself to come home and just want to sleep. I just made sure they ate, took a bath, and went to bed. As I began to come out of such a place, and I was looking back on the last days of those years—yes, it was literally years—it was like wandering around in the darkness. I was like a dead person and no one knew. Months and years passed as I functioned in severe depression outside of my home. There were days people would recognize I was a little sad, I know. Yet they never witnessed the side from home. I made a conscious effort to never let anyone see me in such a place outside my home.

For me, as a parent with chronic severe depression, being in such a place rendered me immovable. It was as if I just felt like I could not come out. I had no energy for anything. I had no energy to be a parent, I had no energy to be a source. I had no energy to be a niece, no energy to be a granddaughter. I had no energy for anything requiring effort outside of my normal 9-to-5 job. I DID NOT HAVE THE ENERGY OR WANT TO BE A PARENT IN SUCH A DARK PLACE AS SEVERE DEPRESSION. Looking back at the actions or the lack of actions, to me it was no different than a drug addict or an alcoholic, because I functioned in a place of no parental progression.

It was 2018 when I decided I needed help. I went to my doctor and said, "I am going insane, I have got to do something." She calmly talked me through the crying, prescribed me an antidepressant and referred me to a therapist. At that point, I didn't care what anyone thought about it, I needed help. *I was literally in a fight for my life.* I went to a new church and I loved the way the pastor taught, so I became engrossed in learning more about the Bible, specifically learning more about the price that Jesus paid for us. Just learning was my interest at the start. For years, God would speak through me to others. They would even tell me and try to help me see. I would brush it off and go back into my dark place. It was in 2018 when I first heard the story of Elijah in depth. I learned about the depression he faced. I learned not only about how God wanted him to be honest and open with him about how he felt, but also that God will send someone in the flesh in some form during those times to help us through.

In 2019, when I began to come out of "the dark place," it was not even intentional. I had no desire to move. I had weight loss surgery due to health reasons. I was forced to deal with my "issues" because I couldn't eat them away anymore. No interest was given to actually trying to get better. After all, every time I did, I ended right back up there. During this time, committing to getting closer to God, it was then I took a special interest in Paul and Peter. I began to seek messages, and read my Bible, read commentary, and listen to messages specifically centered around the "coming out" in the Word of God. It was a message one day being taught at church. In the teaching, Pastor spoke about Paul as he recounted all his accomplishments. He talked about how Paul spoke regarding all he had accomplished meaning nothing when it came to God. I began to think on this statement. Why was I working so hard to be this and that? What was I running from? This helped me start to see the light. It helped me not to be told just to pray about it or told it would be OK. My focus shifted from 'this is just the way I am' to 'I am an overcomer, and my children are too.' I began to crave the Word of God.

The first time I was able to tell my children I loved them verbally, I think it was a shock to them just as much as it was to me. As a parent living with Chronic Severe Depression, it takes a daily conscious effort to wake up and be a parent. One of the most rewarding things I have learned on this journey is there is no perfect parent. We all have off days; we all are going to do and say things at times in frustration we wish we could take back every now and then. Own it, forgive it, ask for forgiveness, try to ensure it does not happen again and move on. By trying to ensure it doesn't happen again, I learned to pay close attention to HOW I speak to my children. I learned to allow my children to be children and not expect them to think in my adult mindset. Shoot, I am sure I didn't at their age.

Forgiveness is vital in the journey of depression. Forgiveness is a hard place for anyone. We all have suffered with forgiveness in some form or another. The place I was in, I knew I had to be forgiven by my children. I had to forgive myself as a parent. I remember wondering what mother even thinks about killing herself and her children. Let me explain this: When a mother or person is in such a place, the love for her children and the fear of them living in this world without her, the fear of what someone will do to them if she leaves them on this earth, can easily convince an already depressed mother that if she is going to commit suicide the best thing she can do is take her children with her to protect them. As I began to come out of the dark place, the devil kept reminding me of these thoughts and how horrible I was as a mother simply because I even thought of this. However, what the devil did not remind me of was is that I was ill, I was depressed, and I was not even thinking clearly in those times. Once I was able to grasp this one truth—when I was able to understand, regardless of depression, I am accountable for my thoughts and actions, yet God forgives, and I must forgive myself—God forgave me when I began to ask and draw to him. I had to forgive me to stop the devil from holding my mind captive in those thoughts. Once I decided to no longer let guilt, shame and embarrassment control the place of deliverance I was in, forgiveness came easy and the light became brighter!

I had to forgive their fathers and own my foolishness in however the situation turned out. However, with my daughter it was different. As time passed, her father matured beyond the abusive person I was in a relationship with. Seeing the growth in him as a person and father helped me with my ability to forgive him and love my daughter in a much healthier way. My depression was worst when dealing with my daughter. I knew where it came from. I knew the abuse I suffered at the hands of her father rooted a sense of resentment and regret I had to get past to move forward in my journey out of depression. I wanted so badly to have a mother-daughter relationship, but in a dark place of depression it was impossible. It was impossible to look at her and be happy then. Oh, but when the light started to shine...while I loved her in the dark place, I admire and love her more deeply, without resentment, in the place of light. It is refreshing and guiltless to love her now. The great aspect of it was they were still young so I could start to change the narrative. I could rewrite the story, so to speak. I noticed myself laughing with my oldest son as he told me silly stuff while I cooked.

I engaged in conversation with my daughter, encouraging her to always be the better person when she was talking my ear off about drama at school, instead of snapping and wishing she would hush. Now, I am able to go home, cook dinner, go for a run, sit up with my kids and have a conversation that is not just me fussing. I have kids going into preteen and teenage years, so my focus shifted from fussing at the two to talking to them, helping them to understand whatever the situation is, I am their mother and I love them. For some those things are natural; for us it was new and exciting.

Really surrendering to God and the weight loss surgery helped me recognize and forced me to deal with the root of the underlying issues associated with, and those things which triggered, my depression. I still have days and I still have times I can feel myself sinking due to different triggers. Being out of my routine for days triggers my anxiety and depression. I had to learn this. This is not easy for others to understand. To them, I am being mean or those are just my "ways" but to me, remaining in a place of peace is important to help me on the journey to recovery from Severe Depression.

More recently I learned in the words of Prophetess Deona Benson to "get up while it still hurts." I can feel it creeping up on me and I will say, "OK Lord, OK," and I will tell the devil he is a liar. I'm learning to form a real relationship with God where I don't feel like he's a judge but more so, he loves me and wants to be in relationship with me. I can go to him, talk to him, cry to him. Everyone finds their source of strength in different things. There are different coping mechanisms people use. For me, it was the inability to eat my emotions and refocusing on my relationship with the Father. It was realizing being stuck didn't mean I would always be immovable.

I can tell you that it's not going to be a magic fix. What I can tell you is, as a parent who suffers with severe chronic depression, IT DOES GET BETTER. If you feel like you need professional help, SEEK IT AND FIND IT! Fight every day to find a way to find joy in something dealing with your kids. There is a light at the end of the tunnel. Learn your triggers and recognize when something has triggered those familiar emotions. While others saw someone with this blessed, strong parenting life, we saw some dark days in our house.

Now I'm able to see those blessings. After six years of darkness, I walk in a light that sometimes may flicker but it does not go dark. If ever it does again, I can look back and know I have been in such a place before and I am coming out. In shifting my focus in my parenting and shifting my focus for me to actually see it myself, in choosing to see the light regardless of its flickering some days, I learned I am not hateful, I am not mean, I am not a horrible person. I was DEPRESSED. Even in such depression, God still loved me so much he saw fit to bring me and my children out of darkness.

I LEARNED TO GET UP WHILE IT STILL HURTS!

Monica LaBoo Thomas is the mom of a wonderful son, Delante and, the proud wife of business owner Donald Thomas of Thomas Catering. She has a Bachelor's degree in Accounting, works for the Federal Government, bakes homemade cakes, is a Business Manager for Thomas Catering, and a Mary Kay Consultant.

Monica has a helping spirit and loves to see others smile. She has always wanted to help and encourage others. Her Mary Kay career afforded her the opportunity to associate with women from many different lifestyles. She says, "The smile and the feeling of being beautiful when they leave my presence is priceless. It's not just healing on the outside, but healing on the inside."

She believes it is important to know that you are never a victim of your circumstances or your child's circumstances.

Monica works every day to master at least one goal!! She has learned to take no's and turn them into, "not yet". She takes negative experiences and turns them into positive learning experiences.

Monica knows that God has so much in store for her.

Favorite Scriptures:
Luke 7:13 *When the Lord saw her, his heart went out to her and he said, "Don't cry."*

Isiah 41:10 *So do not fear, for I am with you; do not be dismayed, for I am your God. I will strengthen you and help you; I will uphold you with my righteous right hand.*

THE OTHER SIDE OF THE GLASS

MONICA THOMAS

As a single mother, I'd always made sure that I provided for my son. I wanted to be the best role model for him because I was what he saw every day. As a single mother I think we all have had thoughts of how to raise a son and provide guidance in both the mom and the dad role. When he was small, he was always the inquisitive little one. He would always carry around his little blanket. I watched my little boy grow up before my eyes. He was so talented, too. He could look at anything and draw it and was good with numbers. I tried to really encourage his drawing, but I think it was just a passing hobby.

I saw so many great things in my son. As he grew older and started interacting with other kids, I realized that I could no longer shelter him like I wanted to. I remember when he came home from school to tell me that Santa Claus wasn't real. His friend told him that I was Santa. He looked at me, waiting for confirmation that it was true. Feelings of anger ran through me that someone had stolen a part of his innocence and his belief. I confirmed it. I remember the look of disappointment he had in finding out that it was true. Santa wasn't real.

Time had gone by and it was high school graduation day! Wow, what a proud moment to see him walk across the stage with his cap and gown on. He did it! It was now on to the next chapters of his life. He was smart and had the world at his fingers. He dabbled with different employment opportunities to see where he wanted to land. His grandfather had his own construction company so he reached out to him to ask if he could work with him. My dad was elated. He learned a lot from his grandfather and became very comfortable in that field. I was glad my dad was able to give him some of HIS words of wisdom and allow them time to bond. He was his first grandson. One thing I know he inherited from my dad was the eagerness to become self-employed. He speaks so often of becoming a business owner.

Life isn't always about work. We need to relax a little with those we consider friends. My son was more like me and could talk to anyone if he chose to. I'm a people person. I enjoy interacting with others and can do so easily. My son, although he had the personality to draw others too him, was a little more reserved. He was always pleasant and displayed his manners, but if he didn't care for you, he would be cordial and keep it moving. He was never disrespectful; he just didn't believe in being fake.

He was a popular child. The girls adored him and the guys that he brought into his circle became trusted friends. I never understood the level of loyalty that came with those that he called brothers, but I found out. All his close friends called me "Ma!" So with that being said, because I was around them often, they actually felt like part of the family.

You can never predict what might happen when your child leaves your presence. You release them into the world in hopes they return home in the same manner. One evening about a decade and a half ago my son left out to hang out with friends. I always asked, "Where are you going? Who are you going with? How are you getting there? Be careful out there!" I always made sure I had the numbers of the friends' parents. At that time cell phones weren't as prevalent as they are now. This particular evening my son was late coming in the house. I called a few of the parents' numbers, and one of the parents' sons was home. I had thought he was with my son. He told me a few of the guys that he was with, so I just waited for him to come in. I was ready to give it to him. Oh, he was going to hear it. I didn't appreciate him having me staying up worrying like this. I didn't appreciate him not being in the house when he was supposed to. They call that a CURFEW! I was so mad! Then the hours continued to grow, time went past with silence for me. My heart began to beat so loud that I could hear it.

I moved from being angry to feeling scared. I have always been the optimistic one. I give hope, I encourage, I give the positive outlooks…I never let anyone look on the downside. It was my turn to talk to myself. Praying is something that's natural for me. So I prayed and prayed and prayed. I don't really know when or how I fell asleep. The next thing I remember was a phone call. OMG! The sound of the phone ringing at that eerie early morning hour... It was from the Police Department. My son had called to tell me that he had been arrested. I never thought I could go through such a mixed number of emotions, but I did. I went from being relieved at hearing his voice to disbelief he was there to being angry that he allowed this to happen. One thing I had to do at that time despite being on an emotional rollercoaster was to listen. I needed answers.

If you have someone in jail, they will never feel comfortable talking normally. You will get the condensed version, and sometimes be left to fill in the missing pieces. That's mostly because all the calls are monitored. As my son began to tell me what happened and provided enough details for me to understand what happened I just went numb. I remember feeling so sad that he was there. All the boys! These boys that called me "Ma!" I thought to myself, *He's in jail!* I called my mom and told her, and she was just as devastated as I was. We both knew that we had to get him out of there. I couldn't think of anything else but trying to get my son back home. So I contacted who I thought was one of the best attorneys. It's important that I let you know, it wasn't that the crime committed wasn't important to me because it was. It's just at that moment, I went into savior mode and I felt like I could get to the bottom of this face-to-face. He needed to be home. We both waited for the bail hearing. I prayed to GOD for a fair bail hearing despite the crime. Who does that? Who asks GOD to forgive a child who deliberately committed a crime? Me. His mother!! God granted my request. Bail was set and my son was being released back to me. Now, it begins…

My first thought was to yell, "What the Heck is wrong with you? Are you crazy?! Have you lost your mind?! I didn't raise you like this! Why did you do this?" One of the hardest things to do is to try to keep your composure. I had every right to lose it! I had every right to beat his ass up and down the street and back again.

So I asked, "What happened? Start from the beginning." He told me everything he wanted me to know. I say that because when you have a group of close, tight-knit friends there is always loyalty between friends. He was loyal to his friends even at this cost. So never believe you've got all the facts. Some things will be left between friends. Nevertheless, the information given to me was enough to make me angry. He was sorry that it happened. What started as a prank ended up having consequences for all of them.

After numerous court hearings the day came for him to face up to his offense. He was sentenced to 18 months in the Baltimore County Detention Center. I had a blank stare on my face when the judge gave the sentence. My son turned around and looked at me as the constable put the cuffs on him and took him out of the courtroom. My heart literally sank. I went in the car and cried like a baby. It hurt so badly. How could I get up and go to work every day like everything was okay? Outside of a few family members, no one really knew. I remember on some family holidays they would ask where he was, and I would just say he couldn't make it. Do you think I felt ashamed? Sometimes! Mostly, I felt hurt. I couldn't understand why. Did he ever stop to think that this wouldn't just affect his life, but mine too? Did he even think about what it would do to me? You know every mother wants the best for their child. I set good examples for my son to follow. I graduated from college, we had our own place, I provided stability, and he didn't want for anything. So why? I thought I was the mom who was easy to talk to. I never tried to be "a homegirl" because I was his mother, but I still thought he could tell me anything. So what was the reason for this? Why would any of them want to do this? I never really knew who the initiator was. I only knew that life for me would be quite different for a while.

My son was in jail. I had to accept it and find ways to cope with that fact. Some people may not think it's such a big deal. Some might say it's your son, not you. The reality is yes, it was my son, but I was the mother who loved her son no matter what. So what happened to him in some part I felt happened to me. I asked myself, "Why couldn't I protect this grown young man from making a decision that would affect his life forever?" I asked myself, "Did I do something wrong? Did I provide a life too good for him that he wanted to see how the other side was? Did he feel loved?" Questions…Questions…Questions…

Anyway, the process began with him going through the system. I also got myself acclimated. I opened an account so that I could receive phone calls from the Baltimore County Detention Center. You had to prepay in advance. If you ran out of money for the calls you would not be able to get their calls. It was his first night there and I wondered if he was ok. My mind took me to all the movies that I had seen when someone goes to jail. The rookie's or newbie's first day. You know, the one where you see them walking down the hall past the other inmates with their blanket folded and the guys behind the bars are screaming. I didn't like the feeling. I felt sick to my stomach. I kept saying, "Why? Why is this happening?!" There wasn't anything that I could do about it, but I just really didn't know how to help myself stop worrying. The phone rang. I answered. The recording said, "You have a call from an inmate in the Baltimore County Detention Center. If you would like to accept this call press 1." I pressed 1 and the next voice was my son. I heard, "Hey Ma!"

I learned that time is very limited on those calls. So I asked, "How you doing? You okay? Did you eat? What did you eat? Are you ok (meaning did anybody bother you…okay)?" He answered, but the thing I did most was listen to his voice. I tried to read in between the lines. One thing I know about my son is if anything was wrong, he wasn't going to let me know. He was strong! So I tried to be too. We talked for the allowed time and then he was gone again. He told me they line up to wait for phone time. We talked often on the phone. I would always have my phone so that I wouldn't miss his call. I can tell you, though, after most calls for a while I still cried. My heart hurt so bad. I didn't want him in there. I wanted things to go back to normal. My mind always played tricks with me. So I did what I knew best, and that was to pray. I prayed all the time. Sometimes when I lifted my hands up in prayer to God, I felt someone in my spirit so strong that I thought I could walk on top of water and wouldn't fall. I wanted that hedge of protection around my son. A barrier that couldn't be penetrated. Our phone time became routine.

Going to work in the midst of this was tough for me in the beginning. I really didn't want to work. I couldn't concentrate, but I knew I had a job to do so I did it. I was a likable person, so it wasn't out of the ordinary for friends and co-workers to approach me and boast about the great accomplishments of their children. I would listen and congratulate them. It was a genuine compliment from me. They should boast and be proud. It's a proud mommy moment no matter what age they are. I would have been too. I would have loved to boast. They would ask me how my son was doing and what he was doing. I would just say, "He's doing ok." I didn't lie. I changed the subject. I mean really, what was I supposed to say? "Oh, he's in jail!" My son wasn't any different than theirs. He was smart, incredibly talented, and had the ability to do whatever he set his mind to. He just made the wrong detour. I found myself comparing my son to other people's sons and then I stopped. He made the wrong decision and sometimes friends can play a part in that. It didn't alter my love for him. It made me really want to understand more about the "why." Not just the verbal answer given to a question, but the deep underlying reason that made your gut say, "I'm going to do this!" Was it fear that if you didn't your friends wouldn't like you? Was it a cry for attention? Was it because you wanted/needed your father who wasn't a part of your life? I've always been a firm believer that things happen for a reason. Sometimes you like it and sometimes you don't. It may take a day, a month, or years to find out the reason why.

Visiting Day! He was now able to accept visitors. I was glad and anxious to see my son. I wanted to make sure he was ok in the physical aspect, that he didn't have any bruises or marks. You know those darn movies never escaped my mind, no matter how much I tried not to think about it. So when I got in there, I had my jewelry on, my pocketbook, and cell phone with me. I had never been in the jail before, so I didn't know what to expect. It was funny because I thought I could take everything with me. When I went in, I had to wait in line to let the Correctional Officer know that I was there to see my son. I gave his name, my name, and my ID. They told me to have a seat and wait until they called my name. So I sat down in a room full of mixed people of all ages and nationalities and waited. I watched people go through the detector machine and then go to the elevator. Ok…my turn. They called my name. I was walking with my pocketbook on my shoulder and they stopped me. The CO (Correctional Officer) said, "Excuse me, Miss. You can't come in here with that bag." I asked, "So what am I going to do with it?" The CO said, "You can put it in one of those lockers over there." I replied, "Well, if that was the case, why didn't the CO at the desk tell me that? How was I supposed to know?" The CO said, "Miss, you can put your items in there or take them to your car. Come back when you're done!" So I went to the locker and didn't have any change. I was pissed! This lady gave me 50 cents to put my items in the locker. I was ready for Take 2. I walked through and the alarm went off. This time it was my necklace. At that time, I had a gold necklace that I never took off. I believe the clasp was broken so the only way to take it off was to have it cut off. So I explained that to the CO and he just wanded me and let me through. I asked the CO where I should go, and what floor. He said, "Follow the group of people." That wasn't the right answer because some people went to different floors. This one girl overheard my conversation and asked me a few questions and told me my son was probably the same place her boyfriend was. So I followed her.

When I got off the elevator, I had to walk down a long hall. There were rooms with closed doors where I could see someone sitting in them. I assumed they were waiting to see an inmate. The hall seemed to go on forever to me. When we got to the end of the hall we had to walk around the stairs and then we entered another room with three other

COs behind a glass booth. We had to give our names again. So I sat down and waited for them to call my son's name. They would say, "Visit for the inmate's last name."

It was my turn. I had to walk through another booth and then I was in a room with us, the visitors, and the inmates. I saw my son and sat down. The plexiglass separated us, and of course there was the inevitable telephone there to communicate on. I was on the other side of the window looking in. It was good to see his face. I looked him over really good to see if there were any signs of visible trouble, and there wasn't. I picked up the phone and we talked. The CO hollered, "Time's up!" Just like that, it was over. As the months went by, I had become adjusted to my son's new living arrangements, but still had those bad days. We were able to talk often enough and I was able to see him regularly. When he called, I would always ask, "What did you eat today? What is jail food like?" Awful! He would always tell me he made a "hookup." For those of you who know what that is, then you had someone that's been in jail.

My dad died. It was so hard for me. I went completely numb. He had been in the hospital for a while and moved to a nursing home for just a little while to recuperate. He died the day after his birthday. I don't want to talk about this.

I had to tell my son that his grandfather died. It was hard to tell him the news because I knew that he loved his grandfather. It was probably harder on him being inside that place and trying not to show too much emotion. He couldn't even come to the funeral. It gave him something to think about. That, along with everything else, was tough for me. It was during the funeral that those in the family who didn't know about my son being in jail found out. My dad was such a great man. That's all I'm going to say.

The day had finally come. My son would be released, and the rebuilding process would begin. He learned a lot from being there and going through this unfortunate experience. One thing is, he will not go back. Now it's time for him to rebuild and regain trust in society. He will need that to become employed.

I've learned that although we love our children, we can't always protect them from the world as much as we want to. You can't be afraid to let them live, even if some of their experiences take them down the wrong path. I'm looking at this as a learning lesson that he received early in life. For whatever reason he was led down this path, I'm trusting that he will not return there again. I learned that I was stronger than I could have ever imagined. It has made me more aware. To listen more. To love more. Having a child is rich with emotions, uncertainties, joys, and sorrows. I continue to pray. Psalm 121:5 (NLT) says, "The Lord himself watches over you! The Lord stands beside you as your protective shade. The sun will not harm you by day, nor the moon at night."

GOD's got US!

Mary Murrill is a survivor, overcomer, and leader. In 1986, she was the victim of a gunshot that left her paralyzed. She divorced in 2012 and survived breast cancer in 2015. Despite facing such adversity, she never let the trials of life hold her hostage.

In 2012, her tenacity prompted her to seek a degree in Business Management, which she obtained in June 2016. Her passion for liberating entrepreneurs and small business owners from the daily tasks of operating a business prompted her to start her own company.

Mary is the founder of Rescue Me Virtually, a company that collaboratively works with entrepreneurs and small businesses. Her services assist with organizing, maintaining, and marketing the business. Since the inception of her business, Mary has assisted an array of business owners in successfully building their brands. In 2018, she collaboratively wrote her first book, A Threefold Cord Broken: What Happens When Christian Marriages Fail. The book takes you on the journeys of seven courageous Christian women. Each gives a glimpse into their marriage, what went wrong, how they navigated the process as a Christian, how they overcame, the lessons learned, and where they are now.

PARENTING FROM A SEATED POSITION

MARY MURRILL

Becoming a mom is something that I had always dreamed about. When I first found out at the age of 18, being three months pregnant was an excitement for me. Although I was still in school, I was madly in love and knew we were destined to be together. It was my first time on the journey to becoming a mother; the indescribable joy of shopping for new maternity clothes was a new mom's dream.

After a couple of weeks of shopping for maternity clothes and looking at all the cute little baby outfits, I began experiencing a lot of pain and cramping. I immediately contacted the doctor and was told to go to the hospital right away. I frantically called a friend to take me to the hospital. Upon arrival at Providence Hospital in Baltimore Maryland, I was immediately admitted. All during the night, I was in such agonizing pain until finally, I passed a huge blood clot. At last, the pain stopped, with just a little spotting. The next morning, I was released from the hospital. During my discharge, my instructions were to follow up with my obstetrician within the next couple of days. I contacted the doctor's office and, my appointment was set for the following week. Still feeling the excitement of becoming a mom and proudly wearing my maternity clothes, I rode the bus across town for my follow-up visit. Once I met with the doctor and shared my experience in the hospital, she examined me and said, "Everything looks fine and the spotting will lessen over the next few days."

After I got dressed and was preparing to leave, the words she spoke next devastated me. She was offering her sympathy. She said, "I'm sorry you lost the baby." What??!! She said, "No one has told you?" "No!" I said. I had no idea that I lost the baby and none of the doctors or nurses mentioned to me that all the pain I had experienced and the blood clot I passed was a miscarriage. For the next couple of weeks, I went through depression. Although I kept a smile on my face, inside there was nothing but pain. Eventually, I made it through, but that was one of the worst pains I had ever experienced.

A year had gone by and I had already graduated from Mergenthaler Vocational Technical High School (Mervo), located in Baltimore, Maryland. My passion for sewing became my major, Needle Trades. I learned so much about industrial sewing while attending Mervo that I was looking forward to getting a job to use the skills that I acquired. It just so happened that my boyfriend's mother was working at the London Fog sewing factory and she arranged for me to get an interview with human resources. On the day of the interview I was so nervous. Working at London Fog was a big deal back then, especially at the age of 19.

I had only been working my dream job at London Fog for a few months. I quickly advanced in my training and was now qualified to work on the floor with the experienced seamstresses. I was excited to get the position of collar setter. Getting my first bundle of collars was a sign that I could handle being responsible for topstitching the collars and sewing them on coats with accuracy. I would find out later that I would be receiving some more exciting news: I was three months pregnant. Hearing that had me feeling mixed emotions. I was happy and fearful at the same time. I was afraid that if the company found out they would let me go, and happy that I was able to conceive another child. In fear of losing my job I tried to hide my pregnancy as long as I could.

Being pregnant again was my second chance. My boyfriend had a great job and I knew we were destined to get married. I prayed nothing would go wrong. The journey of carrying this child would allow me to experience the joy and pain that mothers go through. I never experienced morning sickness; however, I did have swollen feet and the glow of being pregnant.

Months went by and life was great until things started taking a turn. The wonderful relationship I had was no longer wonderful. I found myself alone, pregnant, and wondering now what I was going to do. In my mind, I had planned on us raising our child together and now I was left alone, doing it by myself. Seven months pregnant, I still found myself trying to get over a broken relationship. While I was at home, doing some work around the house, the phone rang. As I was talking on the phone, I felt a pop on the inside, something subtle, and suddenly a continuous flow of water running down my legs that wouldn't stop. I thought my bladder had released and I was urinating on myself. My mind was racing. What in the world was going on? This was a different experience than when I had a miscarriage. Immediately hanging up from my conversation, I quickly called 911. The ambulance arrived; the paramedics checked me and informed me that my water had broken. They rushed me to Union Memorial Hospital, where I stayed and was placed on a monitor for a couple of days in observation. They gave me medication to delay contractions so the baby would not come too early.

After doing all they could, they were unsuccessful. I was transferred to University of Maryland where they were advanced in delivering premature babies. Within a few hours of being admitted, I was rushed down a long hall to the operating room. This was not supposed to be happening. I was looking forward to having my baby the way everybody else does, with the father in the room, parents and friends waiting in the hall, not being alone in a room full of strangers. My mother was with me at the hospital, but they would not allow her to come into the room due to the severity of the situation. Being in so much fear and not knowing what was going to happen was something I was not prepared for.

On October 7, 1982, I had my firstborn child, my daughter Quieona, weighing in at 3 lbs., 8 oz. As soon as she was birthed into the world, she was whisked away to a ventilator. I never had a chance to lay eyes on her when she was delivered. After I gave birth to her, I was taken back to my room. The feeling of loneliness increased even more. I couldn't see or hold my newborn baby. It took two days before the nurse would come to me and say, "Would you like to see your baby?" No one told me I could go see her, nor did anyone talk to me after I delivered her.

As the nurse rolled me down the hall the anticipation of seeing her increased. When I finally saw her, I was amazed to see how tiny she was. She was just a little bigger than my hand. All I could do was look at her through the incubator and see all of the tubes in her nose that basically covered her face, and the needles in her tiny thin arms and feet that were supplying medication and nutrients to her body. Her lungs were not fully developed, which contributed to her experiencing breathing problems. This is not something I expected from being a new mother. I was not looking forward to being discharged since I couldn't bring her home. I spent many days traveling on the bus back and forth to the hospital. It took a couple of months before I would be able to physically feed her with a tiny bottle. Up until then, I had to pump milk at home and bring it to the hospital for her to be fed through the tube. After a while, that became a challenge because my milk supply started to decrease because my body wasn't producing enough.

For three months, I visited the hospital, praying and anticipating when I would be taking her home. On the day of my last visit the doctor approached me and asked, "Are you ready to take her home?" I was so excited—finally I would be able to enjoy being the mom of a newborn. Since she was a preemie, she had to be monitored on a regular basis. As she grew and began to walk, she started falling a lot more than usual. I wasn't sure why. Her doctor had me set an appointment for her to be evaluated. That's when it was discovered that she had cerebral palsy and was suffering from asthma. Over the years it took a toll on me, going back and forth to the hospital for treatments, evaluations, and therapy. Times were really hard, especially when I reached out to her father for support. He was mainly focused on his career and what he wanted out of life. Although the support provided from both of our parents was there, I did not want to depend on them for what was our responsibility.

Over the years, God has blessed my daughter and me with the strength to get us through. By the time she reached the age of five, much of what she was diagnosed with was almost nonexistent.

As the years had gone by, it had been just the two of us, me and my "mini me." We did everything together, until one day tragedy struck. I was no longer able to spend time with her the way we normally would. Our way of life would be different. While home spending time with two of my cousins and helping one of them sew, our fellowship was interrupted. My oldest cousin was in a dispute with her boyfriend. During a heated conversion, he presented a gun. I proceeded to call the police. The gun went off. I found myself lying on the kitchen floor. I was shot without any warning. I lay on there on floor in disbelief. I was still holding the phone with the dispatcher still on the line. She told me the police were on the way. All I could think of as I lay there waiting was, *I am not going to die. I have a daughter to raise.*

As I was being transported by medevac to University of Maryland, Shock Trauma, the person attending to me was by my side aggressively repeating, "Don't fall asleep!" My response was, "Oh, I'm not falling asleep!" While in the hospital, I found out that I was paralyzed from the waist down and was told that I might not be able to walk again. For some it might have felt like life was lost, but not me. I didn't let that discourage me because I was still happy and excited to be alive!

God blessed me to see my daughter. Although we couldn't have the adventures we had before, we were still able to spend time together, but in a different way. While in the hospital for six months, going through occupational and physical therapy, it made me think about my daughter and how I had to get back to her. By the time I was released from the hospital, I had mastered the technique of driving using hand controls in a vehicle as well getting around by myself in my wheelchair.

In the spring of '86, I was able to move into my first apartment, which was perfect for the two of us. My now four-year-old daughter grew up fast, learning how to clean and prepare small meals. I had good days and bad days, but never to the point where I had her taking care of me. I taught her how to fix meals that were easy and how to properly use a microwave. When we went out shopping in the malls, she would be walking a distance then get restless, I would have her stand on my pedals to catch a ride. If I was unable to reach something high, my daughter would have to get it by standing on the wheels of my chair or the seat. No matter what we did, we made it work.

When she had events at school it became a challenge for me. I had to rely on others to take her and pick her up because some of the chosen venues were not wheelchair accessible. One of the things I hated most was missing out on seeing her progress in ballet and tap dance practices, going on class trips, and allowing her to participate in other activities. It was either a struggle for me to be there or I didn't have anyone else who could help during that time. I remember one time when she was in the 5th grade, she was at the school carnival. I couldn't follow her around to the different games that she wanted to play because I couldn't get across the grass. However, she never once complained about what she couldn't do. Overall, I never had any problems out of her. The only time that I can remember I had to discipline her was when she was around seven or eight. I went to chastise her with a belt, and she ran in the closet. Of course, I couldn't get in the closet, but I tried my best to get in there as much as I could. I was leaning halfway out of my chair, thinking to myself, *You'd better not fall, or you will not be able to get up.* Eventually I was able to catch her. I waited around the corner and kept quiet. Once she didn't realize that I was there she crept out. I snatched her up so quickly that she didn't realize what happened.

By the time she turned 10, she was pretty much doing a lot on her own. My being in a wheelchair became a normal part of our lives and I was glad that the incident did not happen when she was an infant. Over the years, she had matured, and I could entrust her to do a lot of things on her own.

One day as I was in deep thought, looking back over my life, all I could think to do was say, "Thank you, God, for watching over me." Every once in a while, I would think, *Will I ever get married or have more children?* Well, to my surprise, I did get pregnant again. Being pregnant plus being in a wheelchair was equivalent to being pregnant for the first time. I didn't know what to expect. To me the process should be the same, not knowing that the complications from previous times could be even worse now. The damage that the bullet caused could have an impact on whether this would be a full-term pregnancy or if there would be complications in delivery.

God blessed me with a specialist at Sinai Hospital that handled high risk pregnancies. I was one of his last patients before he retired. This time I was totally prepared for this pregnancy. I did everything I was told to make sure I didn't have any problems. My mom was on standby, my best friend had her beeper—everyone was ready. However, things didn't go as planned. This time, I was eight months pregnant and experiencing a fever and chills, and my water broke. I called my mother on the phone, my best friend on her beeper, and couldn't reach either of them. I had to get in touch with another friend to come and give my daughter and me a ride to the hospital. When I arrived, they would not let my daughter go upstairs so she had to stay in the lobby. Once I was settled in my room, the doctor examined me and said the baby was coming and she would need to conduct a C-section. I told her, "No!" She said, "Can you push?" I said "Yes!" Off to the operating room we went. I pushed a couple of times and out he came. Sean was 7 lbs., 11 oz.

Now I had a newborn son and a ten-year-old daughter. I never thought about how I was going to manage. I did know one thing: This was my son, not my daughter's. I was not going to make her responsible for taking care of her baby brother. I was able to enjoy breastfeeding him. I thought it would be impossible to breastfeed him due to the damage caused by the gunshot in my left breast; however, I was still able to produce milk. Whatever I needed to do around the house, my son would be secured on my chest in a carrier or sitting in his swing. When I went to the store, he would once again be secured on my chest while shopping. When finished, I would put the bags in the car, place him in the car seat, then get in the car myself. I used a wheelchair lift to store my wheelchair. With a push of a button, the chair was in the car and off we went.

When it was time to wash him up at the sink, I would lay him on my lap. This one time, however, when he was around three or four months old, I had him on my lap and he rolled off and fell on the floor, in between my chair and sink cabinet. I felt so bad for dropping my baby, thinking I was a terrible mother because I didn't hold him properly. From that day forward, I found a better way to secure him so that would not happen again.

As he grew older and started to crawl, I had to be more watchful. I gave him freedom to move around but also had to give him boundaries. I did not want him to crawl into a space I could not get him out of, especially under the bed. When he began to stand it was even better because now, he could grab onto my chair and it also made it easier for me to pick him up. Now he was big enough to sit up on my lap and ride standing on my pedals. Getting around with both of my kids wasn't too much of a struggle, since they were both young with me being in a wheelchair. It wasn't hard for them to adapt. I never had a problem with them running off or being disobedient.

By the time Sean turned five and Quieona was 15, our lives were getting ready to transition into the next phase of being a family. In early September of 1996, I got married and our family instantly blossomed into a blended family. I was now the mother of five: two girls, ages five and 15, and three boys, ages five, six, and eight. I wasn't sure how it was going to work out, because their mother was still partially involved in their lives. I wasn't trying to replace her; however, I wanted to be a mother figure who would build a relationship with them. Even though they had a mother, they addressed me as "Ma," just like my own kids, and respected me in the same manner. My love for them was the same as my own children; there was no division and I did not treat them any differently. Sometimes I may have done more for them to make sure they didn't feel like they were without. The time I spent with my kids was priceless, taking them to soccer practice, baseball, wrestling, school dances, school parades, plays, cheerleading, various awards, and numerous competitions. I made sure I went to each of their events. Although we did things most families do, I had an encounter that involved making a tough decision.

My next-to-youngest (step)son had problems with retaining information, which made it difficult for him to learn in school. After meeting with the teachers and speaking with the doctors, it was determined that he had ADHD. I had the responsibility of determining whether to put him on medication or not. I was not familiar with ADHD, how it is properly diagnosed, and the side effects of the medication. After gathering all the information to make a sound decision, we decided to try the medication. After taking it for a while he started to complain about his stomach, even though the medication was helping him concentrate more, I did not want him in pain. That's when we were given another medication. After a weekend of using the new medication, he started complaining about having bad headaches. By this time, I was fed up. No more medication! I sat down with his teachers and explained I was not going to subject him to pain because they needed him to concentrate more. The alternatives to this situation were for the teachers to have more one-on-one time with him during class, have him move to the front of class, and have him in more of a group setting. Some teachers would insist children be medicated instead of finding alternative ways to educate them. Well, this was not going to be the case with mine.

Sadly, my marriage came to an end by 2010. I was devastated that I might not see them as much, but I am glad I had an opportunity to be in their lives until they were all 18 and graduated from high school.

I've enjoyed motherhood, with all the trials that came with it. All my kids are now grown. My "mini-me" Quieona is now married and owns her own business. All my children, except for my son Sean, have children. He is pursuing his master's degree.

I pray that what I have instilled in them and showed them from child-hood to becoming adults helps them with becoming better parents.

"There's no way to be
a perfect mother and
a million ways to be a good one."

– Jill Churchill

Perita H. Adams is the mother of one, Antonio. She holds an Associate Degree in International Business, and a Bachelor Degree in Organizational Communications from Wingate University in Charlotte, NC. After completing several Study Abroad programs and missionary work in Africa, Brazil, Montreal, China, Mexico etc., she found a passion for working with women, helping them to develop their gifts and talents as a Christian Life & Business Coach. She is self-employed and is the owner of The GeneSIS Beginning Coaching & Consulting LLC. Since the age of five she has had a passion for creative and technical writing as well as a strong artistic ability. In her down time, she enjoys family time, reading, writing, and traveling.

Contact information:
Perita H. Adams-Certified Christian Life & Business Coach
The GeneSIS Beginning Coaching & Consulting LLC.
10130 Perimeter Parkway
Suite 200
Charlotte, NC 28216
Website: www.thegenesisbeginning.com
Email: thegenesisbeginning@yahoo.com

A MOTHER'S PROMISE

PERITA H. ADAMS

In the Beginning

As a young girl I always felt called to do something great! I wasn't always sure of what that was because whatever I felt God asked me to do, I would try my best to do it. Sounds strange, huh? I was privileged at a young age to know God and I always felt His presence. So I would do things that may have not been so typical of a young girl. You ask what? For example, I would write letters to God about various things I saw going on in the world or with people. I guess you could call them prayers.

At the age of 16, I remember a still, small voice saying, "There is a great number of children whom I love without mothers or fathers, and this deeply saddens me." During the era when I grew up, in the late '70s and early '80s, cable television was a foreign phenomenon. Televisions had very few channels and at least two channels were news related. The typical channels played old Western flicks and your favorite sitcom or show once a week. In fact, you scheduled activities around that day because if you missed it, well, let's say it would be a week before you'd be able to see it again. I bring this up because on Sundays there was a program called *Feed the Children*. Some of you may remember what I'm talking about and for those of you who don't let me recap: The children would usually be in Africa and their bellies would be swollen due to lack of nourishment. Also, flies would whisk around their heads like locusts. It was a very sad program to watch but it was harder to turn the channel. All during the program they would make a plea to send $25 per month to "Feed a Child." In the background you would hear the children crying out in pain and hunger. When you looked at the children you would see skeletons. I WAS SO HURT!! So at the age of 16 I made God a promise that I'd give a child in need a home when I grew up. The deal was that I would have one biological child and one adopted child. That was Perita's Plan. Little did I know God's plan was a little different.

During my pre-teen and teen years, I suffered horribly from endometriosis. You can read my story about my battle with this ailment in the anthology *Down for the Count,* available for purchase on my website. But to give you a snapshot of the ailment, not only did it almost take my life, but it took away my ability to have a biological child by causing infertility. Nevertheless, I battled it, prayed through it, and stood on God's word that I would be a mother.

Fast forward into my young adult years. I met and married the man of my dreams. He was sweet, kind, and loving. I told him of my vision and the issues that I might face on my road to motherhood. As I said, he was a gentleman and understood. In fact, his only remark was "whatever happens, happens." He let me know that whether we had children or not, he loved me. I know you guys are saying, "Aww!" So did I!

Motherhood was still on my radar, and I ended up working for a Cancer Treatment Facility. One of our patients was a foster mother. Go figure! Every time she had an appointment, she would bring babies in and say, "Here is your baby, Perita!" I would hold each and every one of them and love on them while she took chemo. The most special memory I had of her was she would buy a special gift for each one of her foster children. It was a bracelet with their name on it and a cross. As I told you, God had a plan. Nonetheless, my husband and I would try and try and try on our own to have a child. Remember the promise or agreement that I had with God. I would have a biological child and then adopt a child. My plan!!!After all that's fair. Right?

Well, a few years went by. No baby, and my condition was growing worse and worse. So my husband and I decided to see a fertility specialist. Our thought was that it was probably just something minor. They could give me medicine and the chances of me conceiving would go up. I still remember the day we left the doctor's office. My head was down, heartbroken, and endless tears falling from my face. I had been concerned for many years and I had a reason to be. Surgery, tests, and more specialists were in my future. No worries, I can do this. I had a plan. God and I agreed—or did we? My husband and I took it in stride and started the process. A surgery here, a surgery there, maybe one more surgery. Pause. This isn't working, God! Wow! I was tired confused, broken, and lost. What was I missing? Hello God, are you still there?

Sorry guys, I just had a moment and had to take a break...

Let's move on. I know none of you have missed the mark with God, or have you? None of you have questioned Him and said why? I sure did during this trial.

Fast forward: I went to a reproductive endocrinologist, someone who specialized in obstetrics, gynecology, and infertility. Here I was, three or four doctors and me in one room with clipboards, stethoscopes, blood work, needles etc. Okay God, I'm feeling a little uncomfortable; my body is exposed. I want to give life, but I don't think I ever pictured it quite like this. I know you are the "Great Physician" but God, these gynecologists and endocrinologists are starting to scare me. Great, the workup is done, and they see the problem. However, they think they could help me to become a mom. How much?! Okay, in my father's house there are many mansions so in theory that means He's pretty rich, but He never told me to spend this much!

My journey

Matthew 26:39 (NLT)

He went on a little farther and bowed with his face to the ground, praying, "My Father! If it is possible, let this cup of suffering be taken away from me. Yet I want your will to be done, not mine.

I can't begin to tell you the process my body underwent trying to fulfill "MY" dreams of motherhood and the road I had to travel. IVF (In vitro fertilization), a procedure to assist me with the ability to have a child, was super expensive. Experimental drugs, ovulation calendars, egg harvesting, and implantation—I was so ready to let this "cup" of discouragement and disappointment pass me by, and it could have if I had just let go and let God! But I couldn't; I wanted it my way instead of fully surrendering.

To my surprise it worked! I was pregnant. Motherhood was in my sights for the first time. Get excited! In fact, I was but it was short-lived due to an ectopic pregnancy. Wow, it was back to the drawing board but this time I went to God first and understood His way was the best way and although I wouldn't fully understand it. I knew He knew what was best for me. So I let go….

Special Delivery

Psalms 139:13-14 (KJV)
For you created my inmost being; you knit me together in my mother's womb. I will praise thee; for I am fearfully and wonderfully made: marvelous are thy works; and that my soul knoweth right well.

In the storm sometimes we forget that God is there and even though we can't seem to find peace He knows not only where it is but how to make it be still…

Even though I let go of trying to do things my own way and in my own strength I never let go of the promise. The promise that I would give a child in need a chance to be loved and be the kind of mother God knew I would be.

My husband and I began to investigate the adoption process. Because God's word says, my people perish for lack of knowledge, I wanted to be absolutely sure of the dynamics of adoption. Only 25 years old, how were I and my husband going to know every "I" to dot and "t" to cross?

God sent a ram in the bush; a young lawyer who recently wrote a book on adoption took our case and taught us everything he knew: free, legally free, open adoption, closed adoption, home studies, temporary and permanent adoption policies as well as the various state laws regarding adoption because every state's laws were different. Public adoption (where the child was ward of the state) and private adoption (where private agencies placed children). How many of you know when God calls you, he will equip you? I could almost write a book on adoption when we were done.

So here we were; my husband and I filled out the necessary paperwork, had our first home study to make sure we had an adequate place for our "little blessing," and started our classes. I saw her; she was so beautiful, only nine months old and ward of the state. She was in the care of the foster mother from the cancer practice. I counted 10 fingers, 10 toes. Once we finished classes, she would get to come to her forever home with us. Exciting!!

But wait, God is a God of mystery. There was another turn. The Christian Adoption agency we had met with had looked over our file and called us. "Come and get your baby; he's ready to come home." He who? What? When? Where?

Happy but confused, we accepted the call and went to let them know we had already found our baby so we couldn't possibly take this child.

The Book of Tony

Psalm 127:3 (ESV)
Behold, children are a gift of the LORD, The fruit of the womb a reward.

We went into the office to tell them our story. Then I heard a slight cry and looked around the room. In the corner sat a little wicker beach bag. It was big and sturdy. Draped on the side of the basket was a little light blue baby blanket with either teddy bears or baby elephants. I stepped back thinking, *No, I'm hearing things we are in the office.* Just then I heard a muffled "coo." My husband and I looked at each other and then at the secretary. She nodded her head toward the basket.

We walked slowly toward the basket, puzzled, and looked inside. There he was, so tiny, rich caramel skin, beautiful brown eyes that stared at us like he knew us, and shiny slick black hair with whimsical curls on the end. He started kicking, smiling, and laughing all at once.

He was about three months, yet so small. "Why is he so little?" I asked. Well he was premature, but he'll catch up. Not that it really mattered because we had our mind made up. He wasn't the one, or was he?

Well, I held him—you know, just so he wouldn't cry. My husband slipped him right out of my arms because he said he didn't want me to drop him. I know, right? We were lost in the moment! I couldn't hear or see anything but him. My husband walked with him around the room talking baby English, giving him his full attention with a smile no one could wipe from his lips.

Then the secretary caught our attention and brought us back to reality. "Hi, did you guys have something you wanted to discuss?" We did but we forgot. "Can we have a moment?" we asked. *Honey, I think he's a special delivery, a gift from God. Me too. This just feels right. So it's settled. Let's tell her.* "When can he come home with us?" "Not yet, we just wanted to see if there was a fit because he was a preemie; he won't be able to go home for another month or so. If you are sure let's complete his paperwork." We were ecstatic, to say the least. God works in mysterious ways! You see, by the way, my husband's name was Anthony and when we asked if the baby had a name it was "Tony."

The Clapper

Psalm 47:1-2 (NIV)
Clap your hands, all you nations; shout to God with cries of joy. For the LORD Most High is awesome. The great King over all the earth.

When we brought our son home, we knew in advance prematurity could produce signs of delayed development. We just didn't know how much. Tony was a happy baby for the most part but then we started to notice small changes in his attitude. Loud noises startled him and made him cry frantically. He had problems breathing because his lungs were still developing. We ran back and forth to the hospital on a weekly basis. But along with his under-developed lungs came reflux. He couldn't digest his food properly and was allergic to everything: perfumes, detergents, etc.

Lord, what's going on? Now we have the family we always wanted but we can't enjoy it. The E.R. doctors came in. "We have to do emergency surgery. His lungs are filling up rapidly with undigested milk and his lungs aren't mature enough to handle it. The risks are great but there's no choice." Tony was now only eight months. He had started to thrive. He clapped constantly with happiness and excitement almost every day. I knew then he was giving God praise for what he was about to perform. A miracle.

The Ronald McDonald House

John 14:2 (KJV)
In my Father's house are many mansions; If it were not so, I would have told you. I go to prepare a place for you.

We lived 30-35 minutes away from the hospital in Greenville, S.C., which was like a lifetime away when we left Tony. While we were in the waiting room, we got a call from the Ronald McDonald house. I thought it was a joke. Note: Now when you see the plastic collectors at the drive-thru window, know it's real. "We have a room for you and your husband." We went over to the secluded house, which looked like a mansion. Once inside people greeted us. Families from all over. We were escorted to the kitchen, where there was warm food and fellowship. We prayed together, cried together, and held each other up. Just then an elderly lady took me into a room filled with blankets. She held me and presented me with a blanket sewn in love by quilters. I never felt the presence of God quite like this. I thanked her and my husband and I headed to our room. No special bells or whistles, just peace knowing we were five minutes from Tony if he needed us.

Trust – Fear = F.A.I.T.H

Trust in the LORD with all thine heart; and lean not unto thine own understanding. In all thy ways acknowledge him, and he shall direct thy paths. Proverbs 3:5-6 (KJV)

As a young Christian mother, I loved Joyce Meyer. She was powerful and had been through a lot. She always wore these glass-type see-through shoes. Well, I found some similar to hers and when the going got tough, I would put on my Joyce Meyer praise shoes and just start shouting through the house. Pretty funny, huh?! But I did it. I was waiting on God and there was no reason why I couldn't usher him in. God has a sense of humor. My feet hurt when I was done.

I wasn't sure how God was going to save Tony, but I knew he could even though I didn't understand everything that was going on. So I stayed in constant prayer. When the doctors weren't sure, I knew the power of a praying mom! Because I had one. Tony had a bumpy procedure, but he made it through.

Romans 8:31 (NIV)
"What, then, shall we say in response to these things? If God is for us, who can be against us?"

It was time to make Tony's adoption final. Boy, did we have a lot of nay-sayers!! He's sickly. No one will hold it against you if you don't go through with it. He's not your biological child so he will be okay.

Let me just say this to every special needs mother or father out there. God does not make a mistake! It's not your fault! Whatever you did or didn't do, God is a forgiving God. He loves you like no other! No one will truly understand the love that child gives you and you give them! Sometimes I look at these children and see the unconditional love of God. All you have to do is be yourself and give it to God!

When we went into the courtroom, Tony was only a little over 12 months. My husband strolled him in, and I carried the oxygen. Our answer to the judge was a resounding yes! We accepted God's assignment.

Finish the Race

2 Timothy 4:7 (NIV)
I have fought the good fight, I have finished the race, I have kept the faith.

I'd like to say things got easier with time, and for the most part they did! Tony and I went through a lot of health issues and challenges. My husband and I didn't make it. No finger pointing. But we never stopped being great co-parents to Tony, and we still are. Single motherhood was a whole other book. (Wait for it.)

Never let people put labels on your children. "Autism" was a label he never accepted. He graduated from high school, a race we ran and won!

He has since finished two years of community college and has about two more to go. He loves showing God has no limits.

1 Corinthians 9:24 (NIV)
Do you not know that in a race all the runners run, but only one gets the prize? Run in such a way as to get the prize.

Tony was and is my prize. You see, my journey wasn't easy, but it was worth it.

Judges 18-5-6 (NIV)
Then they said to him, "Please inquire of God to learn whether our journey will be successful." The priest answered them, "Go in peace. Your journey has the LORD'S approval."

So you see as mothers, there will be times we have to cry, pray, and seek God in every facet of motherhood. Some of us will be saddened because of infertility but that isn't a no from God. There are many children who need us. Sometimes it's not just about the biological features that make us a mother. It's about our ability to share love to children in need of it. Some mothers will feel guilty because their child is handicapped or has special needs, God is looking for that special gift you have in you that no other mother has. You may be a teen or a 25-year-old mother without a clue about this motherhood journey, but you can make it. Keep seeking God's promise in prayer and with patience. Last, know it's okay to make a mistake; moms are only human.

I dedicate my story to all the moms out there because the mom in me recognizes the beautiful, God-fearing, scratch your eyes out if you mess with mine, hard-working, single mama, grandma, mom in you.

Stay blessed!
Love, Perita

"To the world
you are a Mother,
but to your family
you are the World."

– Unknown

Mildred D. Muhammad is an Award-Winning Global Keynote Speaker, International Expert Speaker for the US Dept of State, Certified Consultant with the US Dept of Justice/Office for Victims of Crime, CNN Contributor, Domestic Abuse Survivor, Certified Domestic Violence Advocate, 6X-Author, Trainer & Educator, traveling and speaking on a national and international platform to discuss her life of terror, abuse and heartache, all while promoting Domestic Violence Awareness and Prevention.

As the ex-wife of the D.C. sniper, John A. Muhammad, Mildred shares the very personal details of her experiences involving fear, abuse and many times, victim-blaming. She shares her expertise on what it's like to be a victim, a survivor and warrior of domestic violence *"without physical scars"* to various conferences, seminars, workshop audiences which include victims and survivors of domestic violence, advocates, law enforcement professionals, therapists, counselors, mental and medical health providers, university and college students as well as conduct military personnel training regarding domestic violence.

She is recognized throughout military communities for championship of the Family Advocacy Program and their mission to educate, promote and end Domestic Violence in Military Communities.

Mildred Muhammad has been interviewed on Oprah: Where Are They Now, Anderson Cooper, Ricki Lake, Katie Couric, Issues with Jane Velez Mitchell, The Mike Huckabee Show, TruTV's In Session, Larry King Live, The Tyra Banks Show, and Good Morning America, and has appeared on BET and other local and national TV interviews. She has also been recognized as "One of the Nation's most powerful advocates for victims and survivors of domestic violence". WROC-TV, Rochester, NY.

HEALING MY CHILDREN THROUGH THEIR DADS' CRIME, TRIAL & EXECUTION

MILDRED D. MUHAMMAD

The events that took place in the DC Metro Area from September 2002 – October 2002 altered our lives forever. The whole region specifically and the whole world in general were traumatized. John Allen Muhammad, the convicted and now executed DC Sniper, was the father of my children. We had three children, a son, John Jr., and two daughters, Salena and Taalibah. It had become my mission to raise my children, to the best of my ability, throughout this ordeal as emotionally balanced as possible. I knew it would be difficult, especially with the community blaming me for this situation. They were looking to me for strength, how they should respond to others and the best way to handle their own emotions. At that point, my only concern was my children. How could I raise my children to accept their dad killed innocent people to cover up the possible murder of their mother? I was determined to see them and myself through this by faith. I knew that Allah was with us through it all. I prayed for Him to put people and resources in place to help us.

The Beginning

After the court issued me a lifetime restraining order, we had to establish visitation, which we did. Every other weekend, a mutual friend would pick the children up from me and take them to him on Friday, then return them on Sunday at 5:00 pm. The first weekend went well. The second weekend, they did not return. They had been taken by their father on a weekend visitation on March 25, 2000 while living in Tacoma, Washington. I did not see them again until September 2001. He had taken them out of the country to Antigua for 18 months. After going to court for an emergency custody hearing, I was granted full custody, permission to leave the state without being charged with kidnapping, and I did not have to tell their father of my plans to leave. We arrived in the DC Metro Area September 2001.

Although we were in a safe place, I continued to look over my shoulder because John said I had become his enemy and as his enemy, he would kill me. My children were distant, scared, and unsure of their future. We were in the process of getting to know each other. They didn't know they were taken, without my permission, by their father. He told them they were on vacation and I was coming later. I explained to them that he was not telling them the truth. To prove that point, I showed them my website, 800 number and different emails I sent to others explaining what happened and requesting assistance in trying to find them. At that moment, I could see in their eyes, they realized I was telling the truth. They sat down to take it all in. Now began the process of healing and getting to know each other. Getting to know each other—I did not know my children and they did not know me. Eighteen months of not knowing what happened to them, what they saw, what they experienced, or how they handled situations. So much time had passed since we had been close to each other...mentally and physically.

I noticed they stared at me when I would come in the room. When I looked at them, they looked away. I would be in the kitchen cooking or cleaning a room; they did not want to approach me. Finally, Taalibah began talking to me. She asked what was for dinner! As I described our dinner, John and Salena began talking to me as well. It was interesting how they felt I wasn't approachable. However, I had come to the conclusion that John, their dad, had spoken so badly of me that they were afraid of me and how I would react. So I learned to allow them to come to me and use that opportunity to open doors of communication that would benefit all of us. My son,

John, did not like me very much, let alone love me. His dad was jealous of our relationship. He would always try to stop me from hugging him, picking him up, talking and listening to him. He felt that I was spending too much time with him. As a baby, when he would cry, he would try to stop me from picking him up. We fought constantly about that. My rationale was I did not bring a child in the world to suffer or to feel unloved. As often as I could, I wanted my son to know that he was loved, appreciated, accepted, and valued by me. His dad chose to be distant at first and finally came around to displaying his love for him as well. With our girls, that was not an issue. He was ready to display his emotions and didn't try to stop me from holding them or picking them up when they cried.

As I was seated on the sofa journaling, my son came to me and asked if I wanted to know what his dad said about me. I said yes. He said, "Dad said you didn't want me. Dad said you loved the girls more than me. Dad said you wanted to live the rest of your life without us and that's why he took us." As he was talking, I was crying inside. I didn't want to begin crying because I felt that would not be a good thing to do at that moment. I asked if he said anything else. He said, "Yes, but it will hurt you." I said, "I'm a big girl; I can take it." He said, "No Mom." I said, "Ok, I'm going to ask you to do me a favor. I'm going to ask you to compare what I do to what your dad said. If you find that I'm doing something he said I would do, talk to me about it so you can understand why I do those things. If you hear something that I'm saying that reminds you of something your dad said about it, talk to me. The only way we are going to get through this situation is with the truth. And I will tell you the truth even if it makes me look bad."

After that conversation, I called for a family meeting. I asked each one, "What can I do to make your life better?" John asked for more time together, Salena asked to help me in the kitchen with cooking, and Taalibah asked that we just talk so she could get to know me better. And that's what we did. I asked them to pick a day out of the week to have a mother/son and mother/daughter day. However, our healing routine, as a family, was every Friday we had pizza and movie night. We enjoyed that most of all. Our healing routine continued until each one went to college. We had gotten to a point where our conversations were more informative. They became comfortable and began sharing their experiences in Antigua. They experienced hopelessness, fear, abandonment, and the fear of where they would end up. However, they knew that they were safe now.

Innocent People Killed

It was September when we first heard of people being shot in the area. It was October when it began on a regular basis. Each day after October 4th, the DMV was anxious. I talked to my children on a daily basis. They were afraid to go to the bus stop; they didn't go outside to play once they came home from school. The FBI gave a profile of the shooters as two Caucasians, in a white box truck.

October 23rd, the FBI & ATF knocked on my door. They wanted me to go to the police station to answer a few questions. Once at the station, they informed me that they were going to name my ex-husband as the DC Sniper and that I was the target! I said, "John?" They asked me if I thought he would do something like that. I looked at a corner in the ceiling, then looked back at the agent and said yes. They asked why I would think that. I said, "We were watching a movie and he said, 'I could take a small city, terrorize it, and they would think it would be a group of people and it would only be me.' I asked him why he would do something like that, and he changed the subject. They said they had to put me in protective custody. I told them we had to go and get my children, sister, and brother-in-law, which we did.

We were taken to a hotel until they caught him. My children were confused, hurt, and shocked the sniper was their dad. The next day, they caught him at a rest stop. A few days later, we watched the news report when they had him handcuffed and led him out of the building down the sidewalk. At that moment, I turned to look at my children. It was obvious that they were in pain. I asked Allah for guidance to help them. I tried to get counseling for them. However, it was a high-profile case. Everyone wanted to be on TV regarding the case.

I was referred to one, we went, and I thought it was working until one day, John didn't want to go. I told him we were going and that was that. When we arrived, the counselor came out of his office and walked right up to John. He asked him if he did as he asked. John moved behind me as if he was hiding from him. I said, "Hold up...what are you talking about?" He said, "I asked John to contact Lee Malvo to get his take on this situation so I could help him to write a book since I know you all don't have any money." I said, "You know what...you're lucky I'm not a cursing woman. We are leaving and will not return." As we were leaving, John began crying, saying, "I'm sorry, I'm sorry." I said, "You don't have to apologize; none of this is your fault." He said, "What are we going to do?" I said, "We're going to the library."

Once there, I found a book on counseling and learned to counsel my children. I needed them to be emotionally balanced children so they would grow up to be emotionally balanced adults. We would have conversations about their dad so they would be able to express themselves without being judged by each other. I told them that I was a safe place for them to talk about their dad without bias and judgment. I told them that I was their best resource regarding their dad. And regardless of the questions they asked, I would tell them the truth, even if it made me look bad.

These were our ground rules:

- Everyone is entitled to their feelings
- We will respect each other's feelings
- We will not criticize, judge, or reject the emotions of the person expressing their feelings
- We will put ourselves in their shoes and be compassionate
- We will love each other through this experience
- We have each other's back

With these rules in place, we began our process of analyzing, accepting, and moving forward. They decided they wanted to watch home movies so I could explain the events on each tape. That was painful for me. But... it wasn't about me. My children needed to be reminded of the dad they knew. So, I pushed my feelings aside to give them the emotional support they were craving. We watched five videos. They enjoyed them all. Their pain had subsided...for a while.

The Trial

Each day of the trial was difficult for my children. Each one was displaying anxiety in a different way. Salena is the middle child and the most sensitive. We were seated on the stairs talking and suddenly she began crying uncontrollably. I asked, "Honey, what's the matter?" She said, "Daddy lied to me." I asked, "About what?" She said, through her tears, "He told me he would always be there for me; he said he would always protect me. He said he would never leave me." I said, "I can protect you." She said, "You're not a man. You can't protect me like daddy. I will never trust a man again in my life." I said, "Hold up, honey. It's not fair to judge all men by the actions of your dad. That's not fair...right?" She said, "Yes ma'am, you're right." I said, "I will think of something to help you in this situation."

I called a friend and his wife in Texas. I explained the situation to them. I told my friend that the fate of all men rested on his shoulders. They needed to be around someone, other than me, who knew their dad from a positive perspective. They needed a balance they were not getting here. So we agreed that they could be with them for the summer and off to Texas they went. This was the first time I allowed them out of my sight since the courts awarded custody to me in September 2001. They were away from the area, which helped in my own healing. A few weeks later, they returned, and our reunion was amazing. It was the best medicine we ever had.

The Verdict

The jury came back with a verdict of guilty. He was sentenced to death. I asked to leave work early so I would be home once my girls arrived to give them the news myself. I saw them coming toward the door. I sat down. They came inside and said, "Hey Ma." I said, "Hey honeys" while giving them a hug. They were laughing and talking to each other while I sat watching them interact with each other.

After they settled down, I said, "Well, the verdict came in today." They stopped their activity, looked at me and said, "What is the verdict?" I said, "He was found guilty and given the death penalty." They looked at each other, with tears in their eyes. Salena asked, "Is he going to be executed today?" I said, "No, not today. There is a process that they must go through before that happens." I explained that since he was given the death penalty, he would have a certain amount of appeals. Once those appeals were exhausted, then they would set the date and he would be executed but that would take a long time. They asked, "What are appeals?" I said, "They will review the case from different angles because his attorneys may have found areas in the trial that were not fair to your dad."

That evening, I explained the same information to John, who was in his first year at Louisiana Tech. I asked if he wanted to come home. He said no, he would stay there. His friends knew the situation and they would help him. I said, "Okay honey." Two weeks before the execution, I called him. I told him this was not the time for us to be separated. I said, "I'm bringing you home." He said, "Okay, thank you."

The Execution

It was the day of the execution, November 10, 2009. John was home from Louisiana Tech. Although Salena and Taalibah wanted to attend school, I convinced them to stay home. The house was quiet. We decided to watch

CNN for the updates. The reporters gave a list of people present with John. My children looked at me. They said, "Wassup with that, Mom?" I said, "The list of people was your dad's decision." John asked, 'Why aren't we on the list?" I said, "I don't know." He asked, "Can we talk to him?" I said, "Let me see what I can do."

I was able to contact John's attorney. He said he would call before John went into the chamber so he could speak with his children. He asked us to wait by the phone. The call never came. I watched a man walk up to the podium. I felt it was done. He announced that John had expired at 9:11. My children went in three different directions. My son left the room and went into the living room to sit in the dark. Taalibah dropped to the floor crying uncontrollably. Salena sat on the sofa crying. I gave each one a few minutes before approaching them. I went to John first. He was still sitting in the dark. I asked him, "Are you okay?" He said, "I'm good, Mom...I'm good." I went to Taalibah. I sat on the floor and held her in my arms as if she was a baby. She looked right into my eyes. She was looking for some kind of compassion from me for her dad, but I had no emotions. When he said to me, "You have become my enemy and as my enemy, I will kill you," I severed all emotional ties to him. Once she saw that I did not have those emotions she was looking for, she stopped crying. As she stood up, I asked her if she was ok because she stopped crying so abruptly. She said, "I'm good Mom...I'm good." Last, I sat beside Salena and pulled her toward me. She said, "Mom, do you understand that Dad was going to kill you? Do you understand that he was going to take you away from us?" I said, "Yes Salena, I know. But he's gone and you have to let go."

They cried themselves to sleep that night. To give them closure, I took them to the funeral so they could see him and spend time with his family. As we moved forward, I told them they could not use their dad and his crimes as an excuse for failure. Today, by Allah's grace and mercy, my children are doing well. They are thriving in their fields and emotionally balanced adults.

"Being a mother is
learning about strengths
you didn't know you had."

– Linda Wooten

Misty Muhammad is a licensed financial educator, trainer, and former homeschooling mother of three amazing children and grandmother of one. She is highly respected in her industry of choice as well as in her community, as she endeavors to make a difference in the lives of all she is connected to. Misty enjoys spending time and having fun with her granddaughter as well as family and friends.

Before her foray into the world of entrepreneurship, Misty was a recognized leader within the Baltimore homeschooling community and served as a mentor to many new homeschooling families, assisting them with navigating the law, seamlessly transitioning from traditional schooling to home, tapping into their creativity, building their confidence as the primary teacher for their children and ensuring they had a successful first year.

After seeing the need within the broader homeschooling community for secular Black families, she founded and started a learning co-op and support group called Family Instructors Schooling at Home (F.I.S.H), which ran successfully for four years.

As a licensed financial educator, Misty works to empower and educate communities on various financial principles. She conducts several seminars and hosts financial literacy events for parents and staff of various schools/daycares, churches, health and wellness fairs and women's gatherings. Misty specializes in creating financial strategies for families and entrepreneurs that are customized and works throughout all cycles of life and transitions. Misty loves providing unlimited support and accountability to her clients, helping them to reach their financial goals and dreams. She has won numerous awards has been a guest on two different Blog Talk Radio shows discussing financial matters for married couples and affianced couples.

Misty has dedicated her life to the upliftment and service of others!

FROM CHILD TO WITH CHILD

MISTY MUHAMMAD

I remember it like it was yesterday. A neighbor knocked on my door. He said his famous words when he's about to be all up in my business. "I'm not tryna be all up in your business, but…"

I rolled my eyes like I always do because I knew he was just being "newsy." I let him continue, "I heard your daughter is pregnant and I didn't think you knew. So I just wanted to come and tell you because I would want to know if it was my child."

I. Was. Speechless. And believe me, this does not happen often. What was I supposed to say? After an awkward pause, I just said, "Okay. Thank you." Part of me didn't know what to think and part of me was livid.

Just to paint the back story, when my daughter was 17, I sent her to live with her father. She had been running away and acting out. Her behavior had caused quite an upset in our home. This behavior had gone on for three years. I was tired. I didn't think any of the drama she caused was fair to me or my two other children who resided in our home, so after yet another night of a broken curfew, a heated exchange and what quickly escalated to a physical altercation between my daughter and me, I simply said, "You gotta go! I refuse to fight you and feed you all at the same damn time!"

Her father, who lived in New Jersey at the time, drove down to pick her up. She lived up north for about eight months. She eventually graduated from high school, which was the goal, and shortly thereafter she and her father relocated to Philadelphia. Things had been going well. My daughter seemed to be thinking about her future. At this time, most of our conversations were about colleges and which career paths she was interested in. She had managed to get accepted into the Art Institute of Philadelphia. Even better, she was awarded enough funds to pay for all her expenses. She entered the fall semester and thoroughly enjoyed college life as in incoming freshman. I remember beaming with pride as I accompanied her to her orientation. My oldest daughter was finally getting on the right track! Or so I thought. Right up until my neighbor shared his news.

I immediately called my daughter and asked her how things had been going. She started excitedly sharing details about school, her classes, her teachers, and classmates. I listened intently. Nothing about a baby. She continued to share with such exuberance. She laughed. I laughed. Finally, I said, "Really? That's so awesome! I'm glad you are having such a great experience. When were you gonna add the part about being pregnant?" To this day, I wish I could've been a fly on the wall. You could hear a pin drop. There was absolutely no sound. I almost thought she hung up, so I asked, "Are you still there?" Still, not a sound.

My darling daughter began to stutter as she muttered, "Umm…I mean… how did you know?" I told her not to worry about that and instructed her to get her father on the phone. The three of us talked and tried to figure out how to process this news. I felt such a spectrum of emotions! Hurt, disappointment, anger—I felt anything except joy and excitement. All the hopes and dreams I had for my daughter, I now felt were somehow impossible. I knew all our lives were about to change. Even worse, I knew my baby was not ready to have a baby! She was 19 and she still had a lot of maturing to do. But here we were. My child was with child. No job. No marketable skills. No husband. No fiancé. No boyfriend. No promises of a future together with someone she could raise a child and build a life with. No nothing. All I could see was how difficult her life was about to become. Her having to drop out of college and work odd or low paying jobs for what would seem like the rest of her life. I thought of every possible negative outcome. I thought of how I would have to assist, financially and otherwise. I ruminated about how all her hopes and dreams would be deferred. I was also scared. At moments, I was downright terrified.

Throughout the early stages of her pregnancy, my daughter and her father had been having some difficulty obtaining prenatal care in Philadelphia, so I arranged for my daughter's travels back and forth from Philadelphia to Baltimore for her to receive medical care, which did not start until she was six months pregnant. This was another factor that had been weighing heavily on me. During her first appointment, her doctor asked a litany of questions about the father, which revealed even more less than desirable details about the whole situation.

Throughout my daughter's pregnancy, I lived two lives. The first was the role of the strong support system for my daughter, all while appearing to stay cool and reassuring her and my parents that everything would work out just fine. In my other life, I was having meltdowns, seemingly on a very regular basis. The meltdowns probably happened more frequently than I would like to admit. There were many days I cried in private wondering where I had failed as a parent. Surely, I had "the talk" many times and had very candid conversations with my children about sex regularly. I just couldn't figure out where I had gone wrong.

I remember I met with an acquaintance for lunch at Panera Bread one afternoon. Somehow, we got on the topic about me becoming a grandmother. I tried with everything in my power to put up a brave exterior, but before I knew it, the tears came streaming down. The young woman tried her best to comfort me and empathize, but I was inconsolable. She said it was okay for me to have these feelings and that to some degree, this is normal when you are the mother of a teenage mother. But I didn't want this normal. Part of me felt like she was right. So many times, as women, we do such an injustice to ourselves, all in the name of being strong. Vulnerability has gotten such a bad rap. We see it as a weakness. So we wear the mask and stuff our feelings, not realizing this attempt to not feel and to be strong is literally killing us. I felt like it was probably okay to visit with my emotions and allow myself to feel, but I had pitched a tent and started living there like it was my permanent residence. I would like to tell you I moved on, but the fact is I continued this dual life of presenting a brave face to my daughter and family and privately breaking down right up until my granddaughter was born.

And then it happened. On July 2, 2016, my teenage daughter became a mother and gave birth to a healthy baby girl, whom I lovingly refer to as My Lil Shuga Drop. In that moment, I was so elated and overjoyed at her arrival. All the anger, worry, frustration, stress, fear, and disappointment suddenly dissipated and it was like it never happened! All I could focus on and see was the beauty and perfection of this new life. In the blink of an eye, all the negative emotions vanished. And they never returned.

Isn't it funny how that happens? It's amazing how that works. How at one point in a process or situation all you can see is tragedy or the negatives and then suddenly, once you've progressed to the other side, those feelings just vanish.

I often reflect on my life and the lessons learned. I've even thanked the Divine from time to time for blessing me with such a teachable spirit. As I reflected on the early years of My Lil Shuga Drop's birth, I took notice of how much joy her presence had brought to my life. I was intrigued as to why I was so upset in the first place. So often in life, particularly when it comes to our emotions, we forget or lose sight of the fact that we a) have a choice and b) that at every point in our lives we exercise that choice to be, do or feel a certain way.

It wasn't until months after my granddaughter's birth that I realized I could've chosen to feel differently about the entire experience. Even though I was careful not to vomit my thoughts and feelings all over my daughter during her pregnancy, I didn't exercise that same degree of care and attention to my own self. I could've been more just to myself. I could've decided that I didn't deserve to put myself through so much inner turmoil because of her decisions.

Ofttimes it is hard for us as parents to separate our parenting from our children's choices. During her pregnancy, I was able to see that my feelings were just that, MY feelings. What I forgot while navigating this process was that I determine or decide the emotional domain that I occupy and more importantly, that my daughter's choices were not reflective of me or my inability to parent her. That's the gag that society plays on us: this need to constantly assume that because our children make poor choices, that somehow this means they did not come from a good home or family. That couldn't be further from the truth. Children come from all types of homes, some more suitable than others, but all children at some point develop a mind of their own, begin to see the world through their own lens and will exercise and advance their own ideas and agendas.

Even as I am constructing this chapter, I do not think it was a coincidence that I was asked to be a part of this project and to write about this topic. Since becoming a grandmother, as you can imagine, I have had friends who have joined the club, some first-timers and some friends that were already grandparents. The one thing we had in common is that their children were college students, like my teenage daughter, or their children hadn't found their footing in life and were not prepared to be parents. In each case, I lovingly asked how they felt. I instinctively knew how they felt. I knew they were dealing with their own brand of hurt, anger and disappointment. Maybe this is why you were led to this chapter. Maybe your teen hasn't made it to college and is younger. Maybe they haven't finished high school, or even scarier, middle school. I'll share with you the same thing I shared with my friends...

It'll be okay! Everything will work out for the best for you, your child, and their child. After your grandchild is born three, six or nine months from now, how do you think you'll feel? In most cases, my friends shared they would probably feel differently about the situation, happy even. My response is usually, "Great! Make a decision to feel that way NOW!"

And that is what I want you to take away from this. You have the power to make up your mind to decide to feel that way now. You can literally choose to reframe the circumstances or situation to feel better about things right now. Why? Because you will be okay. Your child will be okay, and everything will work out for your child's and their child's good. What I am suggesting is that you do not even waste time stressing yourself out. Besides, your child and grandchild will have a much higher propensity toward success with your help, love, encouragement, and reassurance than without. I once read a quote that said sometimes it seems like we're being buried when we're really being planted. I can't think of a situation that is more apropos than your baby having a baby before they are grown.

God does not make mistakes, but people do, which means because your child is human, they will make plenty of mistakes, as did you and I. I am not attempting to normalize or minimize teenage pregnancies, but I am challenging you to feel differently if you find yourself having to navigate these waters. To add even more context, most of the teenage mothers I've ever known since I was in high school have gone on to do great things with their lives. They went on to graduate high school, some attended and graduated from college, established careers, families, successful marriages, and businesses because they had a strong village that supported their endeavors to move beyond their current circumstances and soar. And yes, maybe these teenage mothers had to take detours and their goals and dreams were delayed. However, delayed does not mean denied. Their life will no doubt change, but this is not the end.

I explained to my darling daughter early on that being a single, teenage mother would not be an easy road to tread. And it has not. I have watched her struggle at times and make poor parenting decisions. I have also watched her learn from her mistakes and missteps. I reminded her in the early stages of motherhood that this was the life she chose and that she would feel the weight because I would not absolve her of her decisions. Simply put, grownup decisions come with grownup consequences. She has always known I am here to assist, but I was clear that my role, purpose, and function is to do just that…assist, help, aid, and support.

My Lil Shuga Drop is now four years old. She is the happiest, spunkiest little girl you would ever want to meet. She is well loved and cared for and continues to brighten up my days with her smile, infectious laugh, dimples, and humorous ways. I live for her hugs, kisses, and displays of intelligence. I love every second of every minute of being her Gigi!

My daughter has continued to chart her life's path. She has made a few attempts to go back to school, peppered with periodic stops, and has finally found her niche in cosmetology school. She has found something she enjoys, is good at, is genuinely interested in and passionate about. I admire her tenacity and the strides she has and is taking to build a life for herself and her daughter. I am proud of her. I love her and now we've reached a point in our parent/child relationship where I like her (smile). For as much as I would like to take credit for all the things she is doing right, I know I cannot. The same way I learned the onus is on her for what could be perceived as her failures, I can't take responsibility for her successes. In either case, good or bad, she is the product of her own choices. We cannot save our children from themselves.

From mess to message…
From test to testimony…
From fear to faith…
From tragedy to triumph…
From victim to victor…
From bitter to better…
From hole to whole…
From wounds to wisdom…

This is simply the rhythm of life. Ups and downs. Highs and lows. Peaks and valleys. In parenting and in life, we in no way can ever control what happens, but we can absolutely choose how we will respond. We decide how long we will reside on the hurt side of the spectrum. We also decide when we are ready to shift to the other side and heal. With God on our side, all things are possible, and everything becomes 'figureoutable!' Can you dance to the rhythm of life?

I wish you all the best on your parenting and grandparenting journey!

"Even on the days, you feel
like you are failing, look around.
Your child's smile will
bring you right back up."

– Unknown

Alysa Armstrong-Gibbs is the founder of Alysa Gibbs, LLC, an educational consulting firm based in Delaware and serves clients nationwide. She's a wife, mother, and bonus grandma to 8 wonderful (young) men. Alysa's focus is to ensure that diverse learners are seen, heard, and valued at home, in school and in the community, and that their needs are met without limits, and with dignity and respect. Her extensive experience spans 35+ years in various roles, including nanny, teacher, counselor, school administrator, parent coach, mom, grandma, and advocate.

As a Master IEP Coach, Alysa lends her expertise to families to help them navigate the special education system and the IEP process. She trains families on neurodevelopmental techniques to maximize the cognitive, physical, and nutritional health of their differently-abled children. As a former teacher, she leverages her keen attention to detail to proactively identify the needs of children with diverse needs.

Alysa holds a Degree in Human Services/Child Welfare and is a graduate of Partners in Policymaking. She has garnered accolades for her advocacy work, including winning the Advocate of the Year in 2018. Her work has been featured on radio, TV, podcasts and in magazine articles. She also lends her expertise through speaking engagements, workshops, and conferences. Alysa is proud to serve as a support parent for Parent 2 Parent of Georgia and serves on the Advisory Board for an Atlanta based nonprofit, Our Children's Story.

"ABORT!" THEY SAID

ALYSA ARMSTRONG-GIBBS

There is a side to having a child with special needs that no one wants to talk about. I will.

There I was, an emotional wreck, lying on my closet floor sobbing uncontrollably, when my husband walked in looking for me. I was a "new" mother for the first time in twelve years. Our newborn son was at the hospital in the NICU, where he stayed for nine painstakingly long days.

"What's wrong?" he asked, while he attempted to wipe the tears from my face. As I continued to wail insuppressibly, all I could manage to say was "I'm sorry." With a confused look on his face he said, "Sorry for what?" Feeling completely helpless, I looked in his eyes and answered, "I'm sorry for not giving you the perfect son."

My life up until that point had not gone as planned. Not in the least bit, outside of the fact that my life plan included being married by twenty-one. I was, but it failed miserably a year later. I wanted six children and by now I only had the two boys plus my bonus son. My life consisted of traumas that I had no idea that I could ever triumph over. We are talking divorce, sexual assaults, death of loved ones, and abusive relationships. Now I was remarried and had given my firstborn son a stepfather, a little brother, and just moved him into a new home. I thought, *Wow, things are finally looking up*, but my firstborn and life had different plans.

My husband and I each had a son from a previous relationship. This was our start-over baby. Since I was of advanced age, the doctors wanted to have all the suggested prenatal tests. My initial blood work determined that there was a possibility our child would have Down syndrome. At one of our ultrasound appointments they saw some slow bone growth and the lack of a bridge on his nose. The doctor requested that we have an amniocentesis. We immediately said, "No! Why would we risk the life of our unborn child if we have already decided to accept whatever we are blessed with?"

Doctors, nurses, and support staff put pressure on us to get the additional screening. After we declined, they then put pressure on us to terminate our pregnancy given their initial blood test and ultrasound results. So basically, medical professionals determined that our unborn child's life was not worth living based on a 'maybe!' Without knowing for sure, they had already decided for us, then tried to convince us, that he should be ripped from my "advanced maternal age" body. Selective or genetic abortions happen in roughly four out of every one thousand pregnancies due to some sort of "fetal abnormality." Add Down syndrome to the mix and those numbers skyrocket. The latest statistics reveal that the Down syndrome abortion rate is 100% in Iceland, 98% in Denmark, and almost 90% in the United Kingdom. It's 67-85% in the United States.

That was not going to be our reality. Nothing had changed. We were still determined to carry our baby to term. I had originally planned to continue to work at my job as a teacher until delivery. Unfortunately, in February 2005, two months before his birth, I was found passed out in the parking lot of the school. I was under tremendous stress for months, in part, because of doctors calling me to terminate my pregnancy. They called me often, until my husband called and told them that he would pay them an in-person visit if they continued to call his wife. The calls stopped just shy of the last chance for a legal abortion in Georgia. Bedrest, however, was one of my final directives from the doctor that I did heed.

At one of my regularly scheduled OB/GYN appointments, the doctor had a worried look on his face. He told me to get in my car and drive to the hospital. He insisted that I not go home, not get my birthing bag, but to go straight to the hospital. "What's wrong?" I asked." He replied, "You're losing fluid. You need to get to the hospital now!" He said it with an urgency that I could not ignore.

I had unknowingly been in this position before. My firstborn son was a dry birth. Every bit of fluid was gone, and I didn't know it until the doctor went to break my water and nothing came out. Instead of having my appointment, I drove to the hospital alone. It was decided that they would induce labor. I labored for three days before our son was finally taken by cesarean section. When he arrived, I thought he was beautiful. I thought he was perfect. So why was he whisked away from me? Why was he in the Neonatal Intensive Care (NICU)? Why did he stay for those nine days, hooked up to wires and IV, subjected to genetic testing and treatment for jaundice?

Back to that day, on my closet floor, aboard the hot mess express—my husband told me that there was no need to apologize. He added that he loved our son and that he couldn't be any more perfect. The next thing he said immediately halted my sobbing. He said, "He's gonna be the poster child for Down syndrome! He's gonna do the unexpected."

My breakdown lasted about 20 minutes, but that was the LAST breakdown I had about his diagnosis and the future of my marriage. I quickly sprang into action. With my husband on board, I figured if anybody could do this, I could! My previous employment included being a formally licensed social worker, classroom teacher, mother, and nanny. I was determined to learn everything I could about Trisomy 21, which is the medical term for what people commonly call Down syndrome. My experience with Down syndrome was limited, though I had some. My high school friend, Jenny, had a sister with Down syndrome. Someone who went to my childhood church had Down syndrome. My first cousin's son has Down syndrome. I've worked with students experiencing Down syndrome. I wasn't afraid; this wasn't something foreign to me.

I just needed to make sure that my husband was on board, given the high incidence of divorce in special needs families. We were now officially part of the club "The Lucky Few." I immediately began looking at new ways to redefine our situation. I believe that all children have 'special needs,' meaning they are all neurodivergent. Their brains work uniquely, each in his or her own way. Everyone has their own unique learning styles and preferences. A child doesn't have a disability. They are differently abled. We just said that our son has a different ability; a DIFFABILTY as I began to call it.

Buckle up, Buttercup; here we go....

I researched schools. I signed up for therapies. I relearned basic American Sign Language, so that I could begin teaching him. I found community resources and parenting groups. Unfortunately, there was one huge problem, a problem bigger than Down syndrome in my book. Our baby had a hole in his heart. We were told he'd have to have open heart surgery and he'd have to have it quickly. I did everything that the doctors told me to do. We had to get more weight on him, but eating was troublesome. He couldn't latch on, so breastfeeding was problematic. He suffered with severe reflux and had to be medicated for that. The reflux created a choking hazard and he would often turn blue on us. Benjamin, my firstborn son, nursed for a year, until he self-weaned. I intended to nurse any subsequent children that I may have, but I was just not able to nurse this sweet boy. To add insult to injury, he was allergic to all the formulas. The doctors recommended Alimentum, the most expensive, nastiest smelling, vilest stuff on the planet. We did what we had to do.

I co-slept with our newborn, afraid that he would stop breathing or that his heart would stop working. I had to be near him all the time. My supermom spidey senses were on high alert 24 hours a day, seven days a week. I was blessed that I didn't have to work during my pregnancy. My husband retired me and said I'd never have to work again if I didn't want to. He added that my job was to take care of myself and take care of our boys.

Sadly, I didn't have the best luck with medical professionals with my second-born son, first, due to them pushing abortion on me and then when it was time for open heart surgery. I recall sitting there with my husband, in the office of the cardiologist who was going to be performing the surgery, feeling judged. He acted as if there was something wrong with me because I was so calm. I didn't cry. I didn't ask any questions. I merely looked at his hands, studying them closely. I noticed how small they were, and it gave me a sense of relief. My baby was tiny. I wanted to make sure that whoever was going to be cutting on our baby's heart possessed petite, delicate, and highly skilled hands. I was calm, because I had a dream the night before; it was one of the most vivid dreams I've ever had. I wish I could remember it, but it disappeared almost as quickly as I woke up. The message and feeling from that dream remained. I woke up with a sense of peace. I was shown that everything would be OK. You would think that I would've been a bundle of nerves during a surgery, given they had to split open my tiny baby's chest, but I wasn't. I was as cool as a cucumber, unfazed. I don't think the doctor was used to mothers being that way. Of course, when they rolled him away to surgery, I held him a little tighter and gave him a little extra kiss. I knew he'd be back to me in better shape than he was when he left our side. My little Doodles was only four months old when he had his heart repaired. Afterwards, he was stronger, and wasn't turning blue anymore. No longer was I having to rush to our neighbor next door, who happened to be a pediatric nurse at Children's Health care of Atlanta.

We began as quickly as we could with therapies. We enrolled in the Babies Can't Wait Program and our son soon began in-home speech therapy, occupational therapy, and physical therapy. As our lives evened out some and my stressors were somewhat at bay, I began to desire to work again. I missed working with children in a larger group setting. My father agreed to fund the purchase of an after-school enrichment center for me. I was thrilled; working with youth is my superpower. Roughly two weeks into the purchase, and me taking over the program, tragedy struck again. On the morning of June 26, 2006, I left home early with my little Doodles strapped in his car seat. I went out picking up items for the center that I had purchased via Craigslist. On the way back, I noticed a truck headed toward another vehicle spinning wildly out of control. I looked around quickly and saw nowhere for me to go. It was inevitable. I had a true "Jesus take the wheel" moment. I let go of the steering wheel, took my foot off the pedal, turned around to look at my baby in the back seat, then it happened, the impact of a six-car pileup. I spent roughly the next month in the hospital. I had to move my family into my parents' home, have multiple surgeries, rehab, have daily shots in the stomach, and had metal screwed into my leg and ankles to put me back together again. A wheelchair, transfer board, and bedside toilet were now part of my daily existence. Would my life ever get back to normal? Would I be able to take care of my child who needed so much from me? Would my marriage survive this?

Fast forward three years to pre-K. Kashiim was enrolled in a special needs, self-contained classroom. We soon found out that this would not work. Our son was coming home exhibiting behaviors stereotypical of a child on the autism spectrum. Instead of using words to communicate, he would grunt and do lots of arm flapping. We immediately withdrew him from this program. We vowed to seek only fully inclusive environments for him. We found another pre-K classroom housed in a daycare center, and this is where even more problems began. This is where I started honing my advocacy skills. It's hard to talk about how I found him, one day at pick up. I walked in and could not find my son. Someone motioned to the bathroom and once I got there, I found him on the floor, soaked in urine and surrounded by feces. He was saying "Mommy, bathroom my poop." He said no one would help him. I have no idea how long my son was in that bathroom alone. I had no idea why no one helped him, but I knew that neither full inclusion nor my son was valued at that facility. I reported the facility, which went out of business shortly after. I then found the Holy Grail of inclusion schools in Georgia. We found Coralwood. We enrolled him for another year of Pre-K and ended up doing two years of kindergarten there as well. There he received the best public education he's ever had. Don't get me wrong; we still had a fight. We had to push for that second year of kindergarten. We even had to push to get him in there to begin with. We spent the next few years in public school fighting for proper accommodations, modifications, services, and higher expectations for our son. While in elementary school he made the honor roll and principal's list. He even had his art highlighted in an art show. Still, after an exhausting third grade year, we pulled him out to homeschool. Honestly, I was just tired of the fight. We had to fight everywhere for acceptance—in the community, at the doctor's office, at the school.

Once we began homeschooling, our life had a renewed sense of freedom that I never thought possible. My husband has afforded us the ability to travel freely, keep me home with our son fulltime and oversee his private therapy sessions, and for our son to pursue his dreams. Kashiim has been able to take music, art, and theatre classes and swim lessons. He was chosen to be a brand ambassador for Gigi's Playhouse Atlanta and represented them over several years at their annual fundraising gala. He's had a newspaper article written about him and has even appeared in the magazine *Good Housekeeping*. Our son has been in about six fashion shows from coast to coast and met people from other countries as he participated in programs with professional dancers and musicians. He has been personally coached by an international professional model and shot by an international photographer, both of which have graced the pages of Vogue. We are blessed.

My life may not be perfect, but it is mine. My son is doing well and is considered one of the success stories. He is the poster child for what is possible with Down syndrome. We have even been asked to go to Africa and train other moms of children with Down syndrome. Kashiim has his own Facebook and Instagram page and is working on a book titled *Get Ready With Me* where he teaches adolescent boys about the importance of routines and hygiene. On any given day you can find him playing Xbox, working out, playing his favorite music, practicing for his next fashion show, or talking to friends and family on his phone. He is a typical teen. He is excited to learn how to drive a car, about the start of high school, and about revamping his website for his business. His dream is to get married, own his own large house, and have many children. I won't stand in his way.

I won't let myself, family, society, or himself put any limits on him. Like him, I can't put limits on myself. Like the famous poem by Langston Hughes, "Life for me ain't been no crystal stair." You know that mythical bird, the phoenix, that rises from the ashes reborn? Well, imagine I am that glorious bird, but then someone comes along and douses me with gasoline and then throws a match. Yeah, that! But I am here to say that no matter what has been thrown at me—car crashes, failed health, weight gain, parenting struggles, divorce and threats of divorce, being a victim of police brutality, failed life goals—I am STILL here. I'm that mom who will sit in the car for a half hour before going inside. I will cry in the shower. Sometimes I am hanging on by a thread. Sometimes I am barely treading water.

BUT the difference between me and those who stay and wallow in it is that I give it a time limit. I must get up and move quickly. If I need to break down, I allow it. I feel it fully then move on within 10 minutes, or an hour or a day at the most. If I fail, I fail forward! I now have new goals that I quickly accomplish. There is no pity party here. Oftentimes, a woman, especially a black woman, is valued for how much burden she can bear. Black women seem to be the example of the epitome of sacrifice and unfulfilled dreams. But I am my mother's daughter, and echoing Maya Angelou, here I stand, "a woman, a phenomenal woman, that is me."

"Taking care of yourself
is part of taking care of your kids"

– Unknown

Cheryl Pullins is a lipstick-loving icon maker who empowers women to unapologetically align all their passions into a distinct brand that takes their business and bank account from humdrum to "iconic Haute-ness."

Leveraging her twenty-plus years of corporate experience combined with a love for film, fashion, and fantastic music, Cheryl has been dubbed, The Icon of Branding. She is a Personal Brand Strategist, an award-winning international speaker with a TEDx stage credit, author of What Every Diva Must Know About Starting Her Own Business, and a Certified Professional Coach who has been featured across multiple platforms and has served as a mentor for the London-based Cherie Blair Foundation for Women in Business.

Known for her stylish and elegant approach to branding, Cheryl is also the creator of the Iconic Woman Lifestyle brand, and the Creative Force + Founder of Iconic Persona™ a boutique premium personal brand development consultancy that caters exclusively to multi-passionate creative women entrepreneurs.

However, even with all of that Cheryl's main passion is focused on working with women who are motivated and ready to discover their I.C.O.N. Factor™ – the secret sauce that empowers them to believe boldly, show up authentically, and live fabulously from their highest potential.

THEN CAME MONDAY MORNING

CHERYL PULLINS

"Mrs. Griffin." That was my married name at the time. "You're on bed rest until the baby is born."

"What?!"

It was summertime in Philadelphia. Who wants to be on bed rest in the summertime in Philly? I mean, have you ever heard Will Smith's "Summertime" anthem?

That's real-life summer in the city, and I was going to miss that whole vibe.

Seven days before hearing those words something started happening with my body. I was spotting. I didn't think much about it. I told Glenn, my husband at the time, what was happening, and he called the doctor's office. They told him to bring me in to be seen.

We made our way over to see Dr. Bolton, who was Muhammad Ali's brother-in-law, by the way. He was known as one of the best (and finest looking) obstetricians in the city. *What?!* I got some good eyes, and I'm only speaking the truth. He was a handsome gent.

Anyway, he delivered my first daughter and we were back for baby number two.

We arrived at the office for my appointment. They called us to follow the technician into one of the examination rooms where she was going to do an ultrasound. We were all pretty jovial and upbeat. *No worries,* we thought. And so it was. The ultrasound was fine. No problems. "See, look. The baby looks good," the technician said.

To be on the cautious side I was put on bed rest. Since I wasn't feelin' the bed rest thing, I gave a fake laugh and we went about our way.

I don't recall much about the rest of that day or even the rest of the week, for that matter. I was bound to the bed and as much as I like to sleep, that got boring fast.

But *then came Monday morning.*

I woke up to a day that I remember as if it just happened. As much as I write and speak, I rarely speak of the day that played out like a self-fulfilling prophecy.

Glenn had taken our daughter Valerye to day care. She was about to turn three years old. While he was out of the house, I was propped up in the bed with a few pillows and eventually I had a deep urge to go to the bathroom, but I was scared to go. Like really scared. I could feel the sensation of the blood gushing and thought, *This can't be good.*

So I sat there until I just couldn't hold it any longer.

We lived in your typical two-story row house in West Philadelphia. It was a bit of a walk down the hallway from our bedroom to the bathroom. I took my time, but it still felt like yuck. I was torn between the feeling of what happens when you can finally go potty and the fear of what could happen when you've been on bed rest for seven days because they think you might lose your baby.

When I walked into the bathroom everything happened fast. While going to the bathroom it felt like something left my body. It just didn't feel right.

"What is happening?" I kept saying. "Oh my God, what is happening?"

I had become hysterical. In my heart I knew what had happened. I had lost my baby in the toilet.

The toilet!

I know what you're thinking. *How did you know you had lost your baby in the toilet?*

All I can say is that a mother knows. My baby had left my body and was floating around in a toilet bowl of bodily waste. My brain was on overdrive. I grabbed a toothbrush and used the handle to swish the dirty water around in the toilet to see if I could see anything, and there it was, my baby. A tiny embryo that didn't stand a chance.

Now here is where I go over the edge.

I was so emotionally distraught I flushed the toilet. However, right after doing it I wailed a cry I had never heard come from my body. It quickly dawned on me that I had flushed my precious baby down the toilet.

Honestly, this moment still brings tears to my eyes and a lump in my throat.

I started walking out of the bathroom and down the hall sobbing so loudly that when my husband came through the door, he said he could hear me outside. I was uncontrollable. He had never seen me like that before and it took him a while to get me to quiet down so I could explain what had happened. Through tear-stained eyes and barely able to catch my breath I replayed the scene all over again. He once again called the doctor's office and they told him to bring me in to be seen.

What Glenn didn't realize is that I was in emotional shock, which is said to be your mind and body's normal way of processing a difficult experience. My reaction to losing my baby in the toilet was too much for me to process so I shut down. I stopped talking, for hours.

Even though I was emotionally checked out, I was still aware of what was happening around me.

Let me give you the scene.

Once again Glenn and I arrived at Dr. Bolton's office. This time things weren't as jovial. Actually, it seemed quite somber. Like they already knew.

Pleasantries were exchanged, but I don't know how pleasant I was. I was most likely more distant than pleasant. Then came time for the ultrasound. This was going to confirm what I already knew. What I didn't share earlier is that when I told Glenn what happened and that I saw the baby in the toilet, he tried to make me feel better by telling me that I *thought* I saw the baby in the toilet, and that everything was going to be just fine.

So there we are in the exam room which is eerily quiet. The technician is doing her thing behind the ultrasound machine. She's looking at the screen and moving the wand around my stomach but doesn't utter a word. In that moment I remembered my ultrasound from the week before. It was the same technician and a week prior she wanted to reassure me that everything was fine with my baby, so much so that she turned the ultrasound machine monitor around so I could see that the baby that was growing inside my womb was just fine and all nestled in Momma's tummy. But this time was different. She didn't turn the monitor around.

She finished the exam, wiped that icky gel off my stomach and told us that the doctor would be in to talk to us.

I was still deep in shock. I had not said anything the whole time while at the doctor's office. Nothing.

Dr. Bolton came in and confirmed what I already knew. I had lost my baby. I heard him, but it was a total blur. This whole thing was devastating to me because I considered myself a healthy woman who had never experienced any woman-stuff complications. My first pregnancy went off without a hitch. Outside of the fact that I gained 50 pounds, I had a cesarean and my daughter was two weeks late, all went well. I delivered an 8 lb., 8 oz. bundle of love. So how in the world did I go from a healthy pregnancy and delivery to losing a baby two years later?

This is where the self-fulfilling prophecy part comes in.

For years I had been saying that I did not want any boys. For some reason I felt that I didn't want to be bothered with raising any sons. I have no idea where that thought came from. I felt like a girl mom, not a boy mom, and apparently, I didn't understand the power of my words. I didn't know that you have what you say. I didn't know that I was a speaking spirit and that I could speak things into existence.

I used my own words to create a future that rocked me to my core, which also left me with the memory of flushing my baby down the toilet. To this day I believe that was my son. You know, the boy I said I never wanted.

This is the first time I have fully reflected on the impact that day had on me. The first time I've walked through the story from end to end. I haven't even gotten to the rest of the story and discovered that I had to breathe through certain parts up until this point. There was definitely some unresolved pain which I had buried deep within myself. Over the past 26 years since having my miscarriage there was one other time where I allowed myself to think about the day when I lost my son, and that was at a women's conference. One of the speakers shared her story about how she lost her baby in the bathroom. This strange feeling came over me and I felt it in my womb. At that point it was 21 years later. Here I am another 5 years after that and I'm finally mentally and emotionally processing every moment of what happened that day.

Speaking of that day, I left you hanging a bit without telling you what happened after Dr. Bolton shared the news with us about our baby. His office was located not too far from the hospital where he had admitting privileges, so he instructed us to go over to the hospital and he would meet us there because I had to have a procedure done.

A procedure? You mean to tell me there is more I have to endure today? That's what I said to myself in my head because I still wasn't talking.

We headed over to Pennsylvania Hospital, which is located in the heart of Center City, Philadelphia. This is where the procedure was going to take place – a D&C. Now, I had heard the term before; however, once again that was something I figured I would never have to concern myself with, but on the contrary, here I was about to have this procedure done.

In case you've never heard of a D&C, it stands for Dilation and Curettage, which is a process used to remove tissue from inside the uterus. In my case it was to clear the uterine lining following my miscarriage.

The room felt cold and sterile. Dr. Bolton walked me through the procedure. I felt like I was about to be lobotomized. I could see the clear tubes and the container where the waste would go once suctioned from my body.

Dr. Bolton had an amazing bedside manner. He was gentle and gracious at the same time. He handled my fragile emotions and bruised heart with care. There I lay, about to be relieved of the final remnants of the evidence of what was left of my pregnancy.

You have probably already asked the question, "How far along were you?" I had just entered my fourth month.

Four months is quite a bit of time when it comes to carrying a baby. Just a couple more weeks and I would have been at the halfway mark and the *mom in me* was having a hard time dealing with the loss of her baby.

After the D&C all I wanted to do was sleep. I needed mental, emotional, and spiritual rest. I was exhausted on all fronts. This was the culmination of a full week of uncertainty and upheaval and rest was not in my immediate future. Once the procedure was done and I got dressed we were told they were admitting me to the hospital for overnight observation to make sure that all was well. That was fine, but the hospital was just about at capacity that day and it seemed like it took forever to assign me to a bed. We sat in the drafty hospital corridor for quite some time. Eventually, I was hungry, and my mouth would have welcomed just about anything at that point.

The evening came and I was finally settled into a room. It had been a long emotional roller coaster of a day and I was drained of the little energy I had left. I'm sure I had some type of dinner which most likely I barely ate and called it a night. I was so over it. I just wanted to go home.

The next day came and I was able to do just that. I went home. What a strange feeling to be pregnant one day and not pregnant the next day. How awkward it felt to spend a full day at the hospital and return home with no evidence of having given birth. Once I walked through the threshold of our house, I was flooded with the memory of what had happened the day before. My emotions bubbled up and my way of dealing with it was not to deal with it at all. I went to sleep.

I don't remember much after that whirlwind of 24 hours had passed. At that point I had worked at my job for about six years and had accumulated enough leave to stay home for a month. I needed the time to heal physically. Emotional healing never entered my mind. I figured it would just handle itself. So instead of dealing with the loss and all the feelings associated with it head–on, I buried the whole thing deep inside of me, thinking it would go away on its own.

Why did I think I could lose a baby and never have to face the emotional aftermath?

Truthfully, I don't know why. I thought it was so common that it was something you would just get over. However, even as I wrote this chapter, I realized that I had not gotten over it, but I had not dealt with it either. It was just lying there in the underbelly of my emotions, waiting to have the Band-Aid ripped off so that healing could take place.

When I started writing this chapter, I got more than halfway through when I had the thought that I should have written about something else. This was too much to deal with. I didn't have time to nurse my emotions and write at the same time; however, what I discovered is that writing about that moment in my life wasn't about ripping off the Band-Aid. It gave me the space to process a pain that I never confronted. It gave me the space to speak openly about how it felt to lose my baby in the toilet. I was also given the opportunity to reflect on how that experience taught me about the power of my words.

There is an incredible deep truth to the power of life and death being in your tongue. Little did I realize that one major thing in my life taught me one of my greatest lessons. If I think about it even deeper the mom in me feels that my baby, the precious embryo of love and joy that left my body on that day, was the conduit used to teach me that there is power in my words.

No, I don't feel guilt or shame for saying I didn't want any boys and eventually losing my baby. The medical staff never had an explanation for why I had a miscarriage. Their only answer was that it happens sometimes.

The body rebels, and I was distraught that it had happened to me, but I was already a mom. I had a daughter and eventually gave birth to another daughter. I don't have any sons and every now and then I find myself saying, "I wish I had a son."

It's amazing how life comes full circle, even when it comes to your words. I am so grateful that I was given the opportunity to share this deeply personal story in this way. My parting words to you, especially if you have experienced this level of emotional trauma: Use my story as a way to heal. Confront what you've buried deep within. It doesn't have to be a miscarriage; it can be anything that you are carrying inside and have not given a voice. I finally gave my pain a voice. I allowed it to be fully expressed, which now gives it the space to heal.

Use your words to speak to the unhealed places in your life. Whether you're a mother, want to be a mother or you're showing up like a mother in someone's life, you have the power of life in your mouth. You have the power to create the very future you desire to live. Start now and use your words to frame your future. Speak life over your children. Speak life over those things which are dead, and you desire for them to live again.

They say the future is in your hands, but never forget that your future is actually in the words you speak. So speak life.

Kelly Freeman-Garrett is a mother, woman of God, wife, friend, and leader who is passionate about developing and inspiring others to become their "best" self, personally and professionally. She was born and raised in Catonsville, Maryland and currently resides in Prince Georges County, Maryland with her husband, daughter, and dog, Rocko. As a mid-level leader and civil servant with the Federal government, she's had the opportunity to live and work abroad. Kelly holds a Master of Public Administration degree from Central Michigan University which influenced and enhanced her leadership skills. An avid reader, Kelly enjoys reading a variety of books to broaden her knowledge, enhance her spiritual growth, and challenge her mind. She's a life learner who believes that various experiences and certain interactions with individuals have allowed her to grow and blessed her with lasting memories and valuable lessons.

OUT OF DARKNESS

KELLY FREEMAN-GARRETT

The summer months brought me delight and joy, and as a child, I had many fond memories of family gatherings and it seemed to last forever. Now, as a working mother, I longed for those days, yet the summer months passed as quickly as an unexpected thunderstorm, quietly causing damage, and cooling the temperatures. In the summer of 2016, my daughter enjoyed a much-needed break after successfully completing her freshman year of high school. I eagerly looked forward to my daughter's sophomore year since she had excelled academically in elementary and middle school and managed to complete her first year with similar success. But a small storm was brewing and would be the start of a journey I never could have anticipated.

The beginning of my daughter's sophomore year proved daunting; the amount of homework as an honors student seemed to double and resulted in slight anxiety. She pushed through it day by day, although it took much longer than normal to complete her homework. As a mom, this concerned me and I wanted to "fix it" for her, make it better and make it magically disappear. We talked often during the weekends about her increased workload, how she felt, if she needed tutoring, and what I could do to support her. I offered my advice, hugged her, and encouraged her to do her best. As the days and weeks passed with the same amount of schoolwork and little relief in sight, I noticed my daughter's heightened stress level. I watched her struggle with schoolwork more than usual; the lack of concentration and focus impacted her ability to complete homework. Fall came and went, my daughter's schoolwork load unchanged.

Little did I know a torment was bubbling inside her that would hit her without warning.

Winter was fast approaching, so I looked forward to celebrating the Christmas holiday and getting a break from school and work. I hoped the break would help my daughter get back on track academically, relax and enjoy spending time with family and some friends. Longing to catch up on much-needed rest, she retreated to her bedroom, often listening to music, or watching a popular teen show. This wasn't unusual for her as a self-identified introvert and someone with a small group of friends, so I didn't observe anything alarming in her behavior or attitude at the time. However, early in the fourteen-day break, my daughter's isolation became more apparent, and social interaction with friends and family lessened. On one occasion, she mentioned to me that she didn't feel like herself and struggled to explain why. But quite honestly, I don't know that I was really listening, like *really* listening, to the words she spoke to me. Internally, I'd hoped that what I observed in the slight change in her personality and what she said were just a "thing" that would pass. *Once she's back in school with a routine, she'll be fine*, I thought to myself. *Once she's focused on schoolwork and does not have time to be idle, she'll be fine.* These same statements constantly filled my head, until the weekend before New Year's changed all of it.

On Saturday morning, as I performed some usual household chores and prepared to go grocery shopping, I passed by my daughter's bathroom to check on her. There she stood, her pupils dilated, her gaze stark and staring blankly in the mirror. I was so startled by what I witnessed, for a moment, I didn't know how to react or what to do. So I stood there still, silently in the hallway and watched her, staring straight at nothing. Finally, I gained my composure and moved toward her, but as I did, she moved back and stiffened. I outstretched my arms, hugged her, and held her tight so she knew it would be all right. After I embraced her, she broke down crying like I'd never seen before. She fell limp in my arms, and I sobbed uncontrollably. My daughter's tears were those of fear, anxiety, and exhaustion. Mine were of concern, worry and helplessness.

Out of Darkness

During that entire weekend, my daughter was with my husband and me physically, but her mind was somewhere else. We initially treated her behavior lightly, coped and dealt with her mood changes as best we could and knew how to at the time. My husband was convinced she was being bullied at school, or it was just a phase and she would somehow "snap out of it". I knew better than to think it was either; call it mother's intuition. Feeling out of sorts about what to do, I called the 24/7 healthcare provider's "Ask a Nurse" service and described my daughter's latest episode and change in behavior to the nurse who answered, which prompted her to ask lots of questions. Then she empathetically provided me with a list of mental health resources, psychologists' names, and a crisis hotline number to call if I felt it was needed. My head spinning and a headache ensuing, I thanked her for the information and hung up the phone.

My husband and I monitored my daughter's behavior and mood the rest of the weekend, with no "real" change in her zombie-like state. The following weekday morning, I made several phone calls, repeated the same information, answered the same questions, and realized after every call that there weren't enough pediatric healthcare professionals to meet the needs of child/teen mental health patients. My frustration grew with each voice on the phone that informed me they weren't accepting new patients, only accepted adult patients, or I left a voice message to receive no return phone call. As a last resort, I finally contacted Children's National Medical Center where my daughter had been seen previously and received other medical treatment. After speaking with at least four different individuals in three departments, I reached the outpatient psychology services department. By this point, I was beyond frustrated and just wanted someone to tell me what to do and, most importantly, how soon she could be seen. The young lady who answered the phone was extremely patient and understanding while I repeated my story for what seemed like the hundredth time, and explained the information received from the "Ask a Nurse" provider service. I also requested an appointment as soon as possible and was especially relieved when the young lady informed me that my daughter could be seen within two weeks. But that wouldn't be the end of it.

105

As the holiday break ended and second semester grades were posted, my daughter's behavior and mood remained unchanged. She eventually lost all interest in everything, particularly school, and wanted nothing more than to be left alone in a dark room. She barely made it through the second semester of her sophomore year of high school, both physically and mentally drained. As the mom of a child who previously excelled academically and was usually well-adjusted, I never expected something like this would happen to my daughter, my only daughter. Her name is Kylie. Little did I imagine that this event would be the beginning of her mental illness crisis, our mother-daughter journey. But just like the summers, you never know when a storm is approaching or how long it will last. This is her story.

It was January 2017, two weeks into the new year, two weeks back to school from holiday break, and two weeks until Kylie's 16th birthday, yet it seemed surreal. Over these two weeks, I did my best to remain positive and upbeat, all the while grieving inside. I counted the days and hours until Kylie's appointment with the psychologist, to get a medical diagnosis of her illness. The days and nights dragged; my husband and I constantly checked on Kylie and monitored her mood, not wanting to leave her alone. Leading up to her appointment with the psychologist, both of us were anxious, not knowing what to expect and hoping to find out the illness that robbed Kylie of her sweet, gentle personality. Neither of us slept well the weeks prior and it was equally challenging to get Kylie up for school; all motivation was gone.

On the day of Kylie's appointment, the January air was crisp and the temperature chilly. I was anxious and nervous. I picked her up from school early, and as we drove to Children's National Medical Center, Washington, DC, we rode in complete silence. Both of us stared ahead, radio playing, and the mom in me quietly prayed to God for guidance and strength. We arrived in the parking garage, stepped slowly out of the car and walked calmly to the hospital entrance to check in. As we walked down the long corridor, I admired the drawings and paintings on the wall and tried to ease the tension both of us felt by doing a silly dance. A small grin appeared on her face. As we waited for the elevator, I sensed Kylie's anxiety building and everything appeared to move in slow motion. We stepped off the elevator and into the waiting area of the outpatient psychology department filled with parents and children—all ages, genders, race. I was surprised to see so many young children under the age of twelve. I signed Kylie in, completed the necessary paperwork, paid the required co-payment, and we waited to be called back to the office to see the psychologist.

"Kylie," I heard the assistant say, "please come with me." She stood and I followed behind her to an office where the nurse completed the intake, getting her height, weight, temperature, confirming her age and briefly asking, "What brings you in today?" Kylie hesitantly answered, "I feel depressed." At that moment, my heart sank, my stomach ached, and I felt nausea. We were led to another office to meet with the psychologist, who greeted us with a smile, introduced herself, and began to share general information.

During this initial visit, the psychologist asked to speak with Kylie and me together, then separately. She also reviewed the twenty-plus pages of new patient forms I completed prior to the visit: family history of mental illness, parent assessment, child assessment, school assessment, and many other questions. As I listened to the psychologist, I kept thinking about how Kylie felt inside. I kept wondering what was going through her head, if she realized the reason for this visit and how knowing her specific illness would change her life. Then the psychologist said these words: "Kylie's illness is major depressive disorder, generalized, and social anxiety disorder, and obsessive-compulsive disorder."

From that point forward, the rest of the day was a blur. I sat stiffly in the psychologist's office; the room spun; I was numb. I tried not to show how completely devastated I was to hear this health news about my daughter, so I pushed past the pain and put on a brave face to keep from crying. I finally regained my composure and asked about treatment, medications, prognosis, and school. This is when I learned the difference between a psychologist, a therapist who provides tools for coping with depressive and anxiety disorders, and a psychiatrist, a health professional who administers the medication in conjunction with therapy to aid in stabilizing the disorders. The psychologist recommended a course of treatment through Cognitive Behavioral Therapy (CBT), and referred us to a psychiatrist colleague at Children's National who would assess and determine medicines suitable to treat Kylie's mental illness diagnosis.

Due to the nature of her mental health state at the time of the visit, the psychologist suggested weekly visits and encouraged the involvement of school administration to coordinate a lighter workload. The appointment with the psychiatrist was made for the same day as the psychologist the following week, where both doctors consulted with each other and discussed the appropriate treatment plan. The initial and subsequent visits with the psychiatrist focused on prescribing, managing, and adjusting medication to alleviate Kylie's anxiety, anti-depressants, and a sleep aid. Leaving Children's National that chilly day in January, I felt relief knowing what caused Kylie's behavior, isolation, and low energy. Kylie seemed distant, unassuming, scared. We spoke very little about the visit, and after we arrived home all she wanted to do was go to sleep, exhausted by it all, mentally and physically.

The next day, I called Kylie's school without disclosing her mental illness diagnosis and discussed options for decreased workload and requested a class schedule change so more demanding classes were at the end of the school day. Kylie worked with the school's guidance counselor and class administrator and rearranged her class schedule; however, I had to speak with teachers individually about coursework and workload. At that moment, Kylie was adamant about not disclosing her mental illness. She was embarrassed and didn't want to be treated differently. If I knew then what I know and realize now about mental illness stigma in the black community, I would've spoken up sooner. The mom in me wanted nothing more than to tell Kylie's story, I listened to her and didn't.

Over the course of two months in therapy and regularly taking her medication, Kylie seemed stable. Then, in early March, her depression deepened, her anxiety increased, and her OCD was more elevated than before. Kylie hit bottom. Her mental illness took a toll on her mind, body and soul. Every aspect of Kylie's life was impacted. The mental illness wreaked havoc on her body, and it starved from lack of sleep, poor diet, loss of appetite, weight loss, nutrient deficiency, female and hormonal imbalances, and pure exhaustion. During the March visits, the psychologist and psychiatrist determined and recommended additional, intensive psychiatric treatment in an inpatient or outpatient adolescent psychiatric program. My heart sank as I watched Kylie, slumped in the office chair staring, no expression or words. She was at the lowest point of her depressive state, and as a mom I felt completely helpless and hopeless. The psychiatrist provided a referral to a program in the surrounding area of our residence, and the entire process proved incredibly challenging and lengthy.

The next phase of the journey began on a March evening in the emergency psychiatric services department of a local county hospital, where an intake nurse and on-duty physician completed a psychiatric assessment and evaluation on Kylie. This initial step of her being admitted to a fourteen-day outpatient adolescent behavioral health partial hospitalization program took hours. Overwhelmed and exhausted, we finally left the emergency room and arrived home close to midnight.

My husband and I struggled with the decision to admit Kylie to the partial hospitalization program, although we knew it was for her safety and ultimately her overall health. She was not at all happy with attending the program and initially resisted, giving in only because this was the option that allowed her to return home each day. By this point, the school administrators were fully aware of Kylie's mental illness, the extent of it, and the effect it had on her. As a family, we adjusted to the new normal; I threw myself into work since this is the one area of my life I controlled, Kylie did what she needed to do to get through each day, and my husband supported her the best way he knew how. We functioned in slow motion while the rest of the world kept going at full speed.

The outpatient program helped Kylie become more connected, be open to talk more about her feelings, and appeared to ease some of her anxiety and fears. Throughout the outpatient program, I remained in constant contact with Kylie's school counselor, class administrator, and psychologist, all of whom showed concern and empathy. Kylie completed the outpatient program with noted progress, but still had a long way to go. Outpatient follow up was provided by a health liaison at Project Phoenix who shared aftercare resources for Kylie. I disclosed her mental illness to teachers so they were informed and understood the reason for the change in Kylie's demeanor. Despite the support of administrators and teachers, Kylie lacked interest and motivation to complete schoolwork and had no energy to get out of bed, get dressed, and regularly attend school. So I reluctantly stopped forcing her to and decided for her sake and mine to let it be. I often read the scripture on a stand in my house which reminded me to just be humble before the Lord. I breathed a sigh of relief when the school year ended. Kylie had completed less than twenty-five percent of the fourth quarter. I dreaded hearing from the school that she would have to attend summer school, but God is good. Kylie's grades from the first half of the year would become her final for the year. I cried.

With Kylie's sophomore year behind us, I worried about the summer, which I usually enjoyed and anticipated enthusiastically, but not this time. Kylie wanted nothing more than to stay home in bed. This was not an option. I searched for an activity that piqued her interest, spurred excitement, and brought her some joy. Cooking was the answer. I enrolled her in a teen cooking class in Alexandria, Virginia that proved beneficial. We often cooked together at home and I figured the class provided a healthy outlet for her, connected her with other teens, helped her learn new cooking skills, and lessened her anxiety and depression. I believe the summer of cooking helped save Kylie's life. Many more visits with the psychologist and psychiatrist for medication adjustments, management and therapy sessions, and visits with medical specialists addressed her physical side effects of the illness, and scheduled meetings with the school psychologist prepared her for the following school year.

Over the next few weeks, I lost myself, totally consumed with Kylie's care and well-being. I developed poor diet and sleeping habits and made little attempt at self-care. I researched mental illness resources online, finding Stronger Than My Struggles, which provided me with daily words of encouragement. I also contacted and participated in a local National Alliance on Mental Illness (NAMI) parent support group, where I was comforted by the stories of other parents who shared similar experiences of mental illness. I attended a community mental health workshop sponsored by the University of Maryland Medical System focused on anxiety and depression. There I gained clarity about facts, myths, and other treatment options for Kylie long term.

During the height of Kylie's mental illness, I selfishly thought to myself, *Okay Lord, this cannot be happening, I have work and don't have time to take off. I don't have time to deal with this.* I constantly reminded myself that she needed my help, and this too shall pass. At the same time, I felt totally overwhelmed and frightened, so I prayed often, "Thank you, Lord, for giving me the strength I need to get through this with her. Amen!" I journaled to write what I was afraid to speak. I meditated to find peace. I listened to Joel Osteen radio and repeated the words he spoke during one of his sermons: Keep God First Place.

The real test of my patience and persistence began and ended with Kylie's mental illness at the forefront of my mind. This was our new normal for almost two years. While her mental illness is a part of who she is as a young woman, it does not define her. She successfully graduated high school in May 2019 and received an academic honors cord. As I watched Kylie walk across the stage and receive her diploma, I cried tears of joy, triumph, and love. As a mom going through a journey of mental illness with a teen daughter, I learned important life lessons. I learned to listen, to let go and let God lead me; I learned to pray, practice patience, self-care, and grace, and to accept support from family and friends. The mom in me wanted to be all things to all people and to do it by myself.

Together, with God by our side, Kylie and I walked boldly through this journey into darkness, never expecting to emerge from the experience whole. Today, my beautiful daughter is out of the darkness that held her hostage for most of high school and seeing the light of day before her.

This chapter is dedicated to my daughter Kylie. In memory of my brother Keith Dominic, who lived with mental illness. In gratitude and love for family who supported us throughout our journey: Jacqueline Carter, Lauren Coe, Blair Freeman, Karen Freeman, and Karen Shoultz. Thanks to the school administrators at Frederick Douglass High School, mental health professionals at Children's National Medical Center and adolescent psychiatric outpatient program, and mental health organizations Project Phoenix, NAMI, and University of Maryland Health.

Resources: Maryland Coalition of Families (MCF) for Children's Mental Health

"The natural state of motherhood is unselfishness."

– Jessica Lange

Tamlyn L. Franklin is an author, engineer, certified Image and Etiquette Trainer, and founder of Etiquette Consulting Group International. A believer in the Triple Threat of etiquette: excellence, civility, and graciousness, Tamlyn uses these principles to help individuals obtain social decorum.

For over twenty years, Tamlyn has provided interactive courses for educational institutions, as well as small and large scale businesses, to provide protocol for how to properly navigate through a business meal, to teaching various methods of conflict resolution in the workplace; provided etiquette training for collegiate and professional athletes, to help them smoothly transition into the professional sports domain; trained children, preteens, teens, and young people to increase self-confidence and develop a successful self-image and project it daily; and trained adults and youth groups in religious organizations and not-for-profit institutions on the essentials of dining etiquette.

Tamlyn received her etiquette trainer certification through the "Professional Woman" Network, a national and international consulting organization specializing in professional and career development. Tamlyn has a Bachelor of Science degree in Electrical Engineering and a Master of Business Administration degree.

Tamlyn is the mother of six, grandmother of three, and lives in Maryland.

Published books include, *How to Become an Unstoppable Black Woman*; 5 steps to a positive image in a sea of negative stereotypes, *The Essentials of Dining Etiquette*; A guide to understanding and mastering dining rules and *Common Courtesy is Free; and etiquette handbook 1st edition*.

Contact:
Tamlyn Franklin
The Etiquette Consulting Group International
www.TheEtiquetteConsultingGroup.com
www.theecgi.com
Tamlyn.Franklin@theecgi.com
Business: 410-299-0623

MINE, HIS, THEIRS, AND OURS— OH MY!

TAMLYN FRANKLIN

I'm what? Pregnant. Dear Lord, this cannot be! I am supposed to start college in a few weeks. How am I going to have a baby and start engineering school? Jesus, this cannot be happening! But when I think back to the month following my 19th birthday, the day I learned that I was pregnant, everything that I thought was important, like picking up my best friend and hanging out and going to parties, fizzled out like a carbonated drink gone flat. The moment that my doctor shared the news and uttered my due date of mid-March 1988, a thousand happy and scary thoughts flooded my mind.

I'm going to be a mother. How am I going to finish, let alone start, college? Should I get married? I was raised by my mom and dad and my close-knit extended family, which included my grandma and great-grandparents. I felt that my pregnancy would disappoint my entire family. *How am I going to tell my mom? What is my great grandfather going to think about this? What about work? Will I be able to work? What about my school schedule? What about childcare? What will my grandmother say? What will my siblings think about me having a baby? I am going to be a mother. I'm going to be somebody's mother. What kind of mother will I be?*

The baby living inside me became my focus. But my biggest concern was how I was going to tell my mom. I thought about getting married so that I could do the "right thing." The thought of marriage was fleeting because I felt I was much too young to get married. Besides, shortly after learning that I was pregnant, I and the young man that I had met in my Army

Reserve, who fathered my unborn child, were going in different directions. We had never discussed marriage or anything important relative to raising a family. Getting married at 19 was not a serious consideration.

Having a child out of wedlock was something for which I criticized and judged myself, and worried daily about what my family, immediate and extended, would think of me. When I tried to share the news over the phone with my mom, I was crying uncontrollably. She could hardly understand what I was saying. I hung up the phone, cried, and prayed. My mom rushed home from her job, bolted upstairs to my room, looked at me and locked her eyes with mine. I gave her the news. She told me to dry my eyes, to hold my head high and not to worry about anyone or what anyone had to say about my pregnancy. I quickly accepted the responsibility that would prove to be my sole responsibility after a bit of opposition.

I had to change my plan. I would no longer go to college out of state but would rather attend a local college. I forged ahead with the modified plan to attend the prestigious HBCU, Morgan State University, and complete Army Reserve drills one weekend each month, while I continued to work weekends at the hospital. I became fixated on preparing for my baby. I began to think about what I ate and if it was good for my baby. I put away my party clothes, dancing shoes, and all activities (college sport activities) that teenagers enjoy. I started collecting baby items, clothes, and all sorts of baby furniture: bassinets, cribs, car seats, and diaper bags. I wanted to provide the picture-perfect living space for my unborn child and had an overwhelming desire to be "perfect" for my baby.

I woke up early Friday morning, prepared to take my final exams before the start of Spring Break during my first year of college, but I realized that my bed was wet. I had been under the impression that when a woman's water broke during pregnancy, water would gush out like a punctured water-filled balloon. I did not know that a very slow trickle meant that my water broke and "it was time." I honestly thought I had enough time to rush to school, take three exams before the start of Spring Break, and then go to the hospital to deliver my baby. After I showered, I called my doctor. Dr. T was shocked at my exam-taking proposition and told me to go immediately to the hospital and not even think about going to take those exams. This was one big lesson early on in my motherhood journey: learning that the perfect plan may not always go perfectly, as planned. Motherhood is like learning to play any sport; when you fall down, you don't stay down. You get back up and keep trying.

For the next few years, while I received on-the-job training as a mother, attended school full time, took my son with me to school when other arrangements could not be made, studied with my baby on my shoulder, sitting on my lap, or riding in his stroller across the college campus with me as I attended classes, and worked diligently every weekend at my job, I watched my baby transition from an infant to a toddler. I watched him take his first steps, speak his first words, gain and loose teeth and cry crocodile tears when I had to leave him with anyone while I attended work and/or school. Seeing him cry for me was bittersweet. I felt loved, needed, and wanted by the one being in the entire world who I knew loved me unconditionally, but at the same time, I felt guilty for having to leave him with relatives and other child care providers. My baby brought so much joy to my new world. I just wanted to be a great mother and give my son the best possible life. As my college career was nearing its end, I bought a luggage set, began squirreling away money, and vowed to travel with my son, starting the summer of my junior year with a trip to Disney World. It was one of the proudest moments of my life, planning the trip, making hotel and rental car reservations, and sitting side by side on the airplane during his first airplane ride.

That trip was the beginning of our annual vacations to Florida and other vacation destinations. After my son's 8th birthday, I took him on the trip of all trips—a four-year long trip, so to speak, to another state when I relocated for a job. It was me and him, more than 1700 miles away from everyone and everything we knew. The time away from close friends and family made my bond with my son even stronger.

My son had to start a new school, make new friends in a new neighborhood and at school, and adjust to a totally foreign environment. It was a culture shock for us both as we were 1% minority in our community, at his school and at my new job. But we had each other. He knew that I had his back.

Since it was just him and me, many miles away from everything familiar, we had fun discovering our new favorite restaurants and other dives that became part of our weekly rituals. On weekends we would either meet up with some of my classmates from school, go to the mall, or drive to the inner city to get him a haircut at a barbershop where we would go sometimes just to chat with one of the barbers who we had discovered was from our hometown. We enjoyed driving an hour every Sunday to attend worship service while listening and singing "Melodies from Heaven" by Kirk Franklin or other beloved songs and then having lunch at one of our favorite places.

During our time away, I decided to go back to school to earn my Master's degree. The problem that I faced then was childcare because I did not have the strong family support system that I was accustomed to when we were back home. I had to rely on new friendships that were started upon my arrival in the new state. So after enrolling in evening classes, I had to figure out how I was going to make it happen: leave work, pick up my son from home or school, who I would get to care for him while I was in class, and get to the college campus every week for the next 18 months. Racing from work to take him to someone else seemed too much at the time with late evening classes that ended at 10pm. So I decided that he would go with me. And he did. My classmates, instructors, and the campus security guard got to know him very well. On the day I received my degree I was extremely proud that he/we had managed to survive the long nights, weeks, and the last two years.

During our few years away from family I was in a childhood friendship that turned into a long-distance relationship, with hour-long daily conversations about everything under the sun. After a few years of dating long distance, frequent plane rides and both of us gallivanting across the country for planned and surprise dates, one of his surprise visits to see me resulted in me becoming pregnant. I was shocked when my doctor told me that I was pregnant and felt the same rush of anxiety that I had felt at age 19. How could I let this happen? He was shocked when I shared the news with him. Our nightly conversations then shifted to how we would move forward. As the baby began to grow inside me, so did my desire to be a great mother to the new baby, my son, and now, his children.

Like me, he had a child while he was in college too. Unlike me, he had gotten married and from their union, he had two children. Sadly, their marriage did not last. Like me, caring for my child, he was living with and caring for the two children from his marriage. When we got married, we went from two individuals living in two separate domiciles with four children between us to a family of seven; his first child, my child, their two children, and our child, all under the same roof. That was a culture shock for everyone involved.

Being blended meant the end of the norm that each of us had grown accustomed to and experienced individually. For starters, when a marriage does not work, the innocent children from the union often feel that they must choose sides with either parent. While that may not be the case, without family or individual counseling, the children have a difficult time adjusting to the separation of their parents and disruption of life as they knew it. Furthermore, the child who grew up being raised by one parent has a very difficult time accepting all the new people now vying for the time of the one parent that they've always had to themselves. The new innocent baby requires time and attention for nursing and nurturing. The new spouses must carve out time for each other, for their marriage, and for their new blended family. Someone, namely the new spouses, must establish their "new norm" regarding spending, saving, meals, school, sports, extracurricular activities, work, childcare, transportation, daily duties and responsibilities, discipline, and disagreements and all the dynamics and emotions swirling around in the new environment. That was an extremely tall order.

My first time going to the grocery store as a new wife and new mom to my new family, I spent more than $500 dollars on every kind of juice, snacks, meats, fruits, vegetables and whatever else you could name. I had it. I was accustomed to almost daily restaurant dining with my son and had no experience buying groceries for a large family. I had not yet learned how to plan a meal based on price per person. When I returned from the grocery store with my infant in tow, all the children helped bring the grocery-filled bags into the house. By the time every box and bag were unpacked, there was not an empty shelf in the refrigerator or the copious cabinets. All my spouse could say was, "Wow!" We laughed about it. In time, I would learn how to shop for us.

With all the needs of an infant, small children, preteen children, and the emotions of being in any relationship, namely a new marriage, it brings about unbearable levels of stress that can cause you to lose your mind or your hair. I'll take hair for $200, Alex. Seriously, I lost most of my hair the first year of marriage. Almost every strand of my hair had fallen out and I wasn't even sure when it happened. I just woke up one morning mortified when I looked in the mirror and all I could see was my scalp. My hair had become as fine as frog hair. It was no laughing matter. I panicked and thought I should get a wig or weave, but I phoned a friend who recommended a stylist and opted to start going to the hair salon to get my hair repaired and began to squeeze in a little "me time," with my baby of course, when the other children were at school.

Blending a family can be a challenge with so many dynamics. Everyone is trying to find their place in the new arrangement. The children had their individual growing pains and discomforts of adjusting to each other. There was sometimes tension between the children who were trying desperately not to get lost in the expansive environment with both parents present, but seemingly far away because both were spread thin trying to give everyone the individual time that they needed and deserved in the "new norm."

One of our children was having difficulty in school. Since I was home with the baby, I thought it would be a good idea to homeschool him to get him back on track. For our lively child, homeschooling required much creativity to keep learning interesting. Everyone was involved in that effort and everything we could do to get him back on track was attempted, including private piano lessons. The homeschool stint was rewarding. I would often find myself standing in our kitchen with a table full of books and other school props, watching as the baby followed behind her brother as he marched around the kitchen table while he completed an assignment. It was a sight to behold and brings back fond memories. That time period required the patience of Job. After a year of completed assignments, lots of patience and recruiting all family members to help, our 4th grader was well equipped to return to public school the following year and private school in the years to come.

Our initial years together were chaotic but early on and throughout, we made every attempt to include everyone in our blended tribe in every activity, whether playing board games, shoveling snow, raking leaves, or a family trip to the local ice cream shop, public library, Little League baseball, football, or basketball game or basketball tournament, local or out of state, dance recital, movie theatre, school event, or attending worship service.

Everyone had to get in where they fit in because it seemed to be constant commotion. While we attempted to have schedules to meet every child's need, the children undoubtedly felt they had to establish themselves or their territory within the home. When the children were amongst themselves, they likely expressed themselves or their concerns in one way or another. One day, the children had a disagreement and with brute force, an apple was thrown at one child by another and mostly landed on the door frame separating the kitchen from the dining room. The hurled apple splattered into over a thousand pieces and stuck to the doorframe, kitchen wall, and backsplash above the stove like it had been finely blended in the food processor and carefully pasted on those surfaces using a spatula.

Thankfully that apple hit the wall but did not hit *anyone*. This incident is one that may not be a big deal but when a family is blended, every tense moment is heightened by the "blended family" undercurrent.

The most painful part of becoming a blended family meant that my one-on-one time with my son was drastically interrupted, and life as he and I knew it had changed. Life as we all knew it radically changed. I can only imagine how each one felt.

Managing a family of seven and after a few years, a family of eight, was like the plate spinning novelty act performed in the circus. It takes a very committed person to keep eight plates spinning simultaneously. There are countless emotions to bear, multiple schedules to manage, numerous people to consider, and various tasks to be accomplished, every day, all while trying to care for yourself and not lose your hair.

While there is no single answer to making it work or avoiding drama, there are three things that I would share that will help every new mother, new wife, or mother-to-be who finds herself in or on the cusp of becoming blended. First, give yourself **time** to learn what the family likes, food choices, budgeting, and scheduling activities. Give yourself time and grace when you make mistakes, because you will make them, and with managing disagreements, discipline, scheduling and delegating chores, and attending or forgetting events. Give yourself time to bond with your spouse; keep a united front and schedule date nights. Give yourself time to bond with your new baby; babies need love, a safe environment, and most importantly, stability. Give yourself time to bond with your new family, both immediate and extended. You might not bond with every family member immediately and everyone involved may or may not bond at all but give it some time. Guaranteed it will not happen overnight, but it can happen, if you give it time.

Secondly, don't be hard on yourself. You may experience frustration and anger and yell or feel like you are in over your head and may even feel guilty for having those thoughts. Those feelings for new mothers and many mothers are not abnormal. You will experience a sea of emotions—joy, sadness, and every feeling in between. You will undoubtedly make blunders, fall asleep when you have other plans, make poor choices, misjudge yourself and others. It's ok. No one is perfect. The sooner you realize that you are not perfect and no one is perfect, the sooner you will begin to appreciate the little things like seeing a child smile, giving or receiving a warm hug from a child, taking an uninterrupted shower, having a heart-to-heart with your friend, child or spouse, celebrating special occasions and other milestones with the family. Just remember to extend some grace to yourself along the way.

Last, make **you** a priority. You have probably heard that you cannot pour from an empty cup and that saying is so true. In my early years, I lost myself trying to care for everyone else. Things happen so fast and time moves so quickly that you rarely have time to make sense of the whirlwind that is your life. Make time to not only prepare healthy meals for your baby and family but nourish your body with nutritious foods and try to refrain from stress eating which can easily pack on the pounds before you realize what has happened. Relieve stress by taking a daily walk before your house starts bustling, or taking a few minutes to meditate and pray, or join and go to the gym (a gym that provides childcare if necessary). Make time with your friends a part of your stress relief. Don't forego time with girlfriends and other family members (i.e., your parents, siblings, other relatives, and friends). Attend family functions, girls' night out, self-improvement classes, workshops, and events. Keep a journal to express your true feelings. Seek outside help if necessary. There is no shame to getting counseling, individual or family, to help you cope with your responsibilities. Continue to grow and develop not only as a mother, girlfriend, or wife, but as a person. You are the only you that will ever be. Your motherly instincts will kick in the moment you give birth or become a mother to other children. Be you and do your best to take care of you as you care for others. Everything will work out for you, if you give yourself time and grace, and make you a priority as you care for others.

As a faith walking fierce champion for women, Traci "Cricket" Crockett has gone from the classroom to coaching to experiencing her own "pause pressing" moments. She is known as a dynamic leader, speaker and storyteller who partners with women to help them dig deep, find clarity and reignite a renewed purpose for their life.

Cricket has a full range of experience. Once an elementary school teacher, she transitioned to rocking it out as a powerhouse direct sales leader and then added Certified Life and Leadership Coach to her list of accomplishments. Cricket has taught, trained, coached, and encouraged thousands of women of all ages to pursue their destiny.

With over 15 years of direct sales experience, building a large team, Cricket uses her voice to share her message at retreats and large conferences. She continues to be a pioneer and advocate for women navigating through their life journey.

Whether in a large or small group setting, or simply one on one, Cricket thrives on being intentional about making deep "iron sharpens iron" connections that are pivotal for the growth and development of women as they walk through every stage of life.

The personal and professional experiences Cricket has acquired as a leader, wife, and mother, have honed her skills to teach, share, lead, encourage and support others

TOTEM POLES

TRACI "CRICKET" CROCKETT

Without warning, your heart and your mind collide with an array of emotions the moment you see those two blue lines... at least that was my experience. I always wanted children, but because of past miscarriages, I was slow to dive in. I was faced with the shock of being pregnant so quickly and the fear of another miscarriage, but as minutes that felt like hours went by, my overwhelming emotion that rose to the top was excitement.

Those two blue lines brought explosions of dreams, hopes, and expectations for my unborn baby and motherhood. It was unintentional, like a baby duck follows its mama. Throughout my pregnancy, and after I gave birth, I continued to dream for my baby. What would it feel like to breast-feed, to rock him to sleep, and experience his first steps? My heart was creating these dreams instantaneously, fast-forwarding to his first day of school, first dance, graduation, wedding day. I had romanticized what it would be like to be by his side as he experienced all these milestones; in some ways these were *our* moments. For the most part my pregnancy was standard, 39 weeks sprinkled with Braxton Hicks and the occasional baby shower. Then just before my due date, I gave birth to a 9.5-pound baby boy. Aside from him being gigantic and slightly jaundiced, he seemed like a perfectly beautiful baby, so imagine my sense of failure when I began to struggle.

The Myth

Sometimes we set ourselves up for failure. We have hopes for our children, but we also create unrealistic expectations for ourselves. Our personal definition of motherhood comes from a variety of things: our own mothers, mothers we knew, iconic mothers from pop culture, or from a place that influenced us like our church or Bible study. Nevertheless, we create expectations for ourselves, for our children, and for parenting in general. Expectations can be alarming because they come out of nowhere, and we don't realize that we have them until they aren't met.

I had an idea of what motherhood was going to look like, but I wasn't giving room to the possibility that God's plan might look quite different. We have a picture in our head, and if things don't happen the way we envision, failure is an easy trap. If we're willing to be open to God, asking, "What do you want me to learn from this?" it's easier to adjust our sails when things don't go the way we hoped. When expectations don't go according to our plan, it's an opportunity to trust and grow in Christ. It's when we push our own agenda that we get in trouble. We are best shaped in the valleys of our lives, not the mountaintops. Somewhere embedded in my thoughts was a script of how motherhood was *supposed* to be, and when I went off script the lie I told myself was *I am a failure*. I didn't have the wisdom in Christ then to consider maybe God was taking me on purpose, for a purpose, in a different direction.

PUSH PAUSE: What are my expectations? Do they align with what God says?

PRAYER: *Lord, help me to seek You. Give me the wisdom to push pause and take stock of my emotions when I get off script. I pray that my thoughts align with your Word.*

The Unexpected

There were several significant events in my life God used to shape me into who I am today. Raising my son was one of them. My husband and I noticed things with our son that didn't fit our expectations as parents. At first, they started out simple like having trouble breast-feeding. Lots of women struggle with this, right? So I didn't see it as a big deal at the time. He was rather fussy, no problem, lots of babies have colic. But what really tipped me over the edge was the fact that he did not like to be held, ever. He would arch his back, scream and cry when I held him. Rocking your baby is the quintessential picture of motherhood, but not for me. Separately these things were no big deal, but combined, I started to feel like a failure as a mother. Our pediatrician tried to reassure me that this was *normal*, but the critic in my head was telling me a different story. That was just the beginning of a long list of expectations for us that would be overreaching at best.

My husband and I realized that we were dealing with more than just "normal" behavior. Red flags continued, and at age 5 our son received his first diagnosis. Somehow, I knew this was going to be the first of many; sure enough, by the time he was 18 he had five diagnoses. With every new year and challenge, I would springboard into *that mom*, trying to find the right plan, the right school, the right medication, the right therapy. I never cared about the labels or the names of what was wrong, I just wanted to know how to be the best mom for him. He was considered high functioning, yet he struggled in every way. He was bullied and it broke my heart to hear him say, "I just want to be normal." Despite his social issues and academic needs, I thought for sure I could help him feel like a "normal" kid and I wore myself out for decades trying.

They say with diagnoses like these, symptoms could get better or worse with puberty; our experience was the latter. Sadly, at 14 he experienced a massive trauma, and life went from difficult to explosive. His emotions became problematic for him to express and control and home life became volatile. At one point, I put my business on hold for years to homeschool him. I did all of this in the name of his diagnoses. I was trying so hard to work <u>with</u> him, but I didn't realize he never adopted my determination or work ethic. He was taking me for granted and I was running us both ragged. Partly because I always created a plan to fix-it, he obtained a victim mentality. One day out of spite, he said to me, "All you've ever done is make me feel broken." Those words still upset me because all I ever wanted him to feel was whole, but I got in the way. I had to learn how to surrender him to the Lord and to stop being his safety net. Why would he ever need a Savior if I was always there to save him? This was beyond hard personally; I longed for support from my mom.

Losing my mom was one of the hardest things I've had to tackle. We were very similar and therefore very close. During my childhood, my father was often gone, climbing the corporate ladder, and so this left my mom and me to bond in numerous ways, some unhealthy. She was the "cool mom" and both I and my friends could talk to her about anything. I appreciated her as my mom and friend, not realizing then the lack of boundaries was detrimental. She was fun and would light up any room, but she had her own demons to slay and many times I ended up being her confidante, friend, and caregiver, rather than her daughter 30 years her junior.

I became a Christian at college. As excited as I was about my new faith, there was an underlying fear of rejection when I told my mom. She was convinced that God was a big, finger-wagging ogre spotlighting her shortcomings. We remained close, but when I talked about anything faith-related, her response was always "You're up on your soapbox." I'd remind her often that God forgave and loved her, but her response was always dismissive. I wanted so badly to share my new life with her, but her shame and guilt would not allow the truth. Throughout the years, she was always there for me, but we could only go ankle-deep because of her unwillingness to talk about faith. That's when God used cancer.

In her late 50s she was diagnosed with a rare blood disorder cancer. Everything went on hold to take care of her and be with her, knowing our time together was fading quickly. My husband willingly became "Mr.

Mom" while I was becoming an honorary nurse for my mom, cleaning PICC lines, checking glucose levels, refilling medications, assessing symptoms, helping after chemo, and advocating with medical staff. While her body was losing its fight, somehow her mind became clearer, sharper, more direct. She became a new mom, grandmother, friend, one I never thought I'd encounter. In an odd way I'm very thankful for those two difficult years.

Near the end of her battle, my husband and I were able to visit her together. On our way I received a phone call urging us to hurry. I was not ready to say goodbye, despite the year and a half warning. As we entered her room, I was shocked to see my mom, not taking her last breath but sitting up in her hospital bed, TV on, flipping through a catalog. When I saw her, I literally fell to my knees and asked, "What are you doing?!" She replied sarcastically, "I wasn't ready to die." While her response was intended to be comical, I took this as an opportunity to push aside my fears and address her faith one last time. With tears in her eyes she took my hand and she said, "I can't explain it, maybe it was just a dream, but I had a moment with God, and I promise you everything is OK." I blurted, "Are you serious right now?!" She was, and later some of her last words were "It is well with my soul." God can use cancer. Because of that conversation, what the enemy meant for death alone, God used for my reassurance and more importantly for her salvation.

It took a long time to grieve her loss. I'm still doing it 20 years later. While I was so glad to know that she fully accepted Christ, and beyond thankful she was no longer suffering, I was not ready to have a life without her. I was not just grieving the loss of a mother; it was complicated. I lost a best friend, a mom, my children's grandmother, and my patient... I recognized even at 20-something that grieving was going to be messy, so I made a cognitive choice to not do it. Sister, if there's something you need to grieve, give yourself permission. Ignoring the pain doesn't mean it's not there. Grief is like a big relentless wave that you just have to ride to the bitter end.

My youngest was born just before my mom passed away and grew up in the shadow of her older brother, but she was easy, fun, and full of joy.

Because our life revolved around our son's challenges, our home was often chaotic, so she learned to stuff her emotions in an effort to not rock the boat. This led to her desire to become *the perfect child*. Consumed with my son, I would check on her: "You'll let me know if you're not OK, right?" She would always reply, "Yes mama," but I was distracted. At the time I was making six figures running my own business, leading a large national team, still trying not to grieve my mom's death, all while trying to advocate like a crazy helicopter parent for my son. I was exhausted and didn't know it. I believed I could handle it all, or at the very least fix it.

We were faced with an opportunity to move back home. We were so excited, but my only hesitation was the timing, the summer before my daughter's senior year of high school. She convinced us she was on-board, and we proceeded. Initially she was thrilled to be the new girl, but eventually the anxiety of not having a consistent friend group set in. The kids from her new school had grown up together and her new student glow was wearing off. Desperate to belong, she decided some friends are better than no friends, even if they're the wrong friends. That choice led her down a crooked path. By the fall, she was simmering like a shaken champagne bottle, while still corked. After years of trying to be the perfect child, she became uncorked.

With a 4.0 GPA, a job, and school commitments, she was working overtime to maintain *the perfect child* façade. My daughter loves to sing and act, so big alarm bells went off when she deliberately didn't show up for a state fine arts competition. When we start to withdraw from the things that we enjoy, we need to pay attention! The problem is, I didn't realize she was withdrawn because she was good at keeping up the act. She wanted to be trusted to take the lead and I was working on not repeating my helicopter mom ways, so when she nonchalantly mentioned her performance was canceled, I trusted her. The next day when she was to perform, my phone blew up with texts and calls asking where she was. We were shocked to find out that she had become so overwhelmed with expectations that she shut down, lied about the piece being canceled, unable to face that the truth would eventually come out. She figured if she couldn't guarantee perfection, why try at all.

It took time to peel back all the layers of what was really going on with my daughter. Through a great Christian counselor she learned the importance of paying attention, something that I had been learning about myself. During the hardest lessons, the ones in the valleys, are processes that we have to carry out our entire lives. Many aren't "one and done" lessons like forgiveness, grief, rewiring negative thought patterns. This time was relatively brief, but during that time she made some decisions I never saw coming, but I had to learn to trust her growth process instead of taking responsibility for her wrong choices. She may have been told to go to counseling, but she chose to be brave there and do the hard work to explore her root issues, becoming more attuned to her needs and thus becoming healthier in the long run.

PUSH PAUSE: How do you deal with the unexpected? Are there circumstances in your life you try to fix? Explore the patterns that lead to this.

PRAYER: *Lord, grant me patience with myself; push pause so I can hear you. I choose to trust you when things seem out of control. Give me the strength to take a step back, be still, and wait on your plan before I activate my own.*

The Crash

I missed all the things that were supposed to happen that never did. This along with all other basic ups and downs became the perfect formula for me to hit rock bottom. I crashed, hard. When life presents a challenge, I create a plan to fix it. This skill is partially due to my personality and upbringing, but also designed as a coping mechanism. But I had reached a point where I couldn't fix it anymore. I was deliberately not paying attention to my warning signs, nor was I truly seeking God's will. My goal was to keep all the spinning plates going. I had the freedom to push pause, examine my wellbeing, and change course, but never knew it or if I did, I was prideful enough to think I was the exception to the rule. I was desperately waiting for someone to see me and give me permission to push pause. Ironically, God already told me to be still and rest.

I spent a lifetime being hypervigilant, anxious, always making sure everything and everyone was OK, excelling in all things because anything less was failure, while refusing to deal with my own traumas. I was like that before motherhood, but these events definitely inflated my habits. I had become a well-oiled machine, never taking the time to consider what I needed to do and more importantly, what God was asking me to do. I didn't make time to pay attention. I'm here to tell you that if you don't deal with your stuff, your stuff will deal with you! I believed that then but didn't think it applied to me. Sister, it applies to all of us!

The crash for me was ugly. I knew it would be that's why I put it off. In doing so, it made this season much harder than necessary. I made a decision to ignore the pain I was feeling. I was "too busy." Girl, busyness is a plague and the enemy uses it to distract us, get us off course, all while we believe the lie that we are being productive (being busy and being productive are not the same!). I'm no therapist, but I have had some good ones, and this is truth: The compulsion to fill our schedules with unnecessary activities is a decision resulting from fear/trauma. These line-items distract us from what's truly going on and if left unresolved, the real issues will grow like a mold. Whether grief is the death of a dream or of a loved one, it shows up at inconvenient times and places. Because I didn't take the time to deal with my issues, I was ill-equipped for life's curveballs.

Imagine wearing a thick, wet, heavy blanket while trying to navigate life. This is how my crash felt. There were days where getting out of bed seemed like running a marathon while wearing 20-pound ankle weights. I would sob for hours. Sometimes the uncontrollable emotion pouring out would concern me, but God's presence was always evident! My crash was a sweet, messy season of surrender, and God was very much with me the entire time. For the first time, I had to get real with my junk, by grieving the losses I tried to ignore, while exploring who He was calling me to be moving forward. It was a time of revelation. It wasn't pretty, but He consoled me while I cried, and He loved me through to the other side.

PUSH PAUSE: Are you running an emotional marathon? Are you vulnerable to the plague of busyness and if so, what can you do to remain healthy?

PRAYER: *Thank you, Lord, that you are my Refuge and my strength, an ever-present help in trouble. Help me to trust you more, to stop wasting time being distracted and worried, or trying to fix it wrestling in my own strength.*

The Truth

The first time I ever went to counseling she asked me about self-care. I had never heard of the term, so I just assumed she meant personal hygiene, but it goes beyond that. Self-care is often misunderstood in Christian culture, and generally there's pushback. According to the dictionary, self-care is "the active role to preserve or improve one's health." I've learned self-care boils down to one's definition. It's more than just "good vibes." I am not encouraging a self-love culture that puts me at the center of my own universe. It's not an indulgence, or doing what makes me happy or feel good, and it certainly doesn't supersede God's word. That is what the church is discouraging and rightfully so. Biblical self-care is not the "treat yo'self" excuse that today's worldly culture encourages.

As Christians we are called to serve others, but the Bible doesn't tell us to neglect ourselves in order to do so. If you neglect taking care of yourself, you're actually impeding your ability to help others. Every time you fly on an airplane, the flight attendant will tell you, "In the event of danger, please put the oxygen mask on yourself first, then your child." Why? In order to give your child the best care, you have to be at your best.

We're to put God first, love others, and serve others. Biblical selfcare is not self-seeking, nor is it self-empowerment, escapism, or blowing off responsibilities. Your body is a temple and you are to take care of it by developing healthy habits, boundaries, and relationships. My definition of self-care is exactly that… taking care of yourself, not gratifying yourself. Self-care is not about making God's Word fit into your belief system, it is seeking His word to transform us.

If you are at risk of heading toward your own crash, it could be because you are low on the totem pole. We use that phrase when discussing priorities. For example, if something is a low priority, we would say it's "low on the totem pole." Friend, I wasn't low on the totem pole, I was nowhere near it! During my difficult seasons, God taught me that I needed to be somewhere on the totem pole. I was not taking care of myself at all. Every single person, place or thing came first and if I had the occasional moment to rest, I felt guilty and selfish. I have learned I must care for my needs so that I'm not pouring from an empty cup. The Word says in Ecclesiastes, "There is a time to weep and a time to laugh," so I had to learn to give myself the time to feel, process, and surrender. I did this by resting, meditating on God's Word, and spending alone time with Him. Jesus himself would often "slip away into the wilderness and pray in seclusion" (Luke 5:16). Likewise, we need to be in community, spending quality time with healthy family and friends, serving and loving others well, and exploring ways to remain mentally healthy too. Hebrews 10:25 says, "Let us not neglect our meeting together, as some people do, but encourage one another, especially now that the day of his return is drawing near."

If you're experiencing fatigue, trouble sleeping, indigestion, frequent headaches, feeling unmotivated, overly emotional, on edge or detached, I would encourage you to speak to your doctor. It could be the sign of burnout or could be something physical like thyroid levels or a vitamin deficiency. Remember sister, you are called to abundant life and that includes feeling better! Your body is a temple and you are called to take care of all of it!

Self-care is more than bubble baths and girls' night out, it's about the growth that happens during the PAUSE. It's things like going to doctor appointments, reading, taking a bath, prayer, exercise, time with "iron sharpening iron" relationships, date night, taking a course, starting a hobby, sitting by the water, Bible study, worship and lots of laughter! The Bible says that a "happy heart is like medicine." You're probably already doing some of these things, now be intentional and pay attention. Self-care will create a healthier you, so you can better serve others.

All my unexpected seasons were sprinkled with unrealistic expectations. I definitely slowed my healing process by not exploring my own self-care. When I began to implement selfcare, learning more about myself and my needs, I became a better wife, mom, and friend. I began to put the oxygen mask on me first. As mothers, we wear many hats, there's a lot of expectations on us, and we add to those expectations as well. Between that and life's curveballs, it's crucial that we push PAUSE, exercising self-care. That way, we can properly assess our physical, mental, and spiritual state. This cannot be accomplished during the plague of busyness but can be done during difficult seasons. The bottom line is, just make sure that you are *somewhere* on the totem pole without compromise! As to where you are to be on the totem pole, well, that's a conversation for you and God.

In Matthew Jesus told us "love the Lord your God with all your heart and all your soul and with all your mind." It's important that your heart, soul, and mind be healthy! You are a whole person, so you need to take care of every aspect of you. Be brave to push pause to fully examine your physical, mental, and spiritual wellbeing. If life gets to be more than you can handle, it's OK to ask for help; that's self-care!

PUSH PAUSE: What is the difference between serving others and putting everyone's needs before my own? Where are you on the totem pole of your life?

PRAYER: *Lord, thank you for your gentle reminder to take care of me so that I can best serve others. Help me to make healthy choices for me with my heart, soul, and mind.*

Felicia Roberts is a native of Atlanta, Georgia. She is a graduate of Spelman College, where she received her bachelor's degree in biochemistry before earning a doctorate degree in Pharmacy from Mercer University College of Pharmacy & Health Sciences.

Felicia always desired to become a business owner, and in 2020 she followed her dream by opening a tearoom in her hometown. Of all her accomplishments, being a mom makes her most proud.

Felicia struggled with infertility for years before finally giving birth to a set of twins. She now uses her testimony to spread encouragement and hope to women experiencing the same journey.

THE CHILDLESS MOTHER

FELICIA ROBERTS

"London just took a turn for the worse. You may want to come see her."
I remember this day as if it were yesterday. October 11, 2015. I was lying
in a hospital bed recovering from just having given birth to my first
child, my daughter London, 36 hours earlier. At 24 weeks pregnant, I
had developed severe early onset pre-eclampsia. My blood pressure was
sky-high, and my vital organs had started shutting down. The only way
for the doctors to save me was to perform an emergency C-section. The
delivery was a success, and my precious baby was in the NICU fighting
for her life. I was hopeful and I was happy. So many years of trying to
conceive, and now I was finally a mom. I had brought a child into this
world. I sat in my hospital bed dreaming of all the good times that lay
ahead for me and my baby – cheering her on at dance recitals, dressing
up for make-believe tea parties, traveling the world together. But when
the doctor rushed into my room and said those words, my fairytale
dreams turned into an instant nightmare.

I immediately jumped out of my bed and waddled down the hall to the
NICU. The next scene I saw would forever be engrained in my memory.
There lay my newly born daughter, my precious baby that I had prayed
so hard for, surrounded by doctors and nurses performing CPR on her
fragile little body. I stood in the middle of the room feeling like I was
in a twilight zone. I was numb. I couldn't believe what was happening.
After minutes of unsuccessful attempts to revive my daughter, a nurse
somberly walked her over and handed her to me. I held her lifeless body
in my arms and I cried hysterically. The nurses had to sit me down and

administer IV meds to calm me down. All I could do was cry and wonder why me? Why my child? The chaplain came in to pray over London and baptized her. I cradled my daughter in my arms, cherishing every second I would be allowed to spend with her. At some point I handed her over to the nurse and walked wearily back to my room.

And this is how my motherhood story began.

Nothing prepares you for losing a child. When you get the exciting news that you're expecting, you immediately start preparing to raise and care for a new baby. You read books, attend new parenting classes, seek advice from family and friends. But there's no manual that gets you ready to handle the loss of your child. There's no chapter in *What To Expect When You're Expecting* that covers the expectation that your baby won't make it home from the hospital. This was the case for me. When I was finally discharged from the hospital my nurse wheeled me outside to be picked up. My wheelchair was parked alongside another new mom going home as well. She waited patiently for her ride with her newborn baby in her lap. Congratulatory balloons and flowers sat beside her. Every few seconds she would gaze down at her new bundle of joy and smile. In my lap sat a box containing my child's footprints, identification tag, and a few memorabilia items with the words *Sleep Sweet Angel* hand-painted on top.

There was no "Welcome Baby" sign on the front door when I arrived home from the hospital. I walked into a cold and empty house. The next few weeks would prove to be the most difficult days of my life. I was still weak and sore from my C-section. I was sad and very depressed. I struggled to find a reason to want to live. All I wanted to do was cry and sleep the pain away. But the mom in me had to find strength to care for my child. Yes, even though my daughter was deceased I still had to provide care for her. I had to plan her final resting arrangements. There were care items requested by the funeral home which I had to deliver. I had to pick out her casket and design her grave marker. I had to go shopping to pick out the first and last outfit she would ever wear.

As much as I wanted to distance myself from the world, I knew at some point I would have to venture back into the public eye. I tried my best to avoid settings where I would potentially meet new people because I dreaded being asked that one question – *Do you have any kids?* I struggled for the longest with how to answer this. None of the stacks of parenting books I had read prepared me for this scenario. What do I say? Am I still a mom? How much information do I divulge to a total stranger? What if I get overemotional and break down crying? I remember the first time I was asked this question. It had only been a few weeks since my daughter's passing, and I had mustered up the strength to go work out at the gym up the street from my home. I was making my way around the circuit room when this older gentleman approached me and started a casual conversation. I could tell by his order of questions what he was leading up to. And when he asked, I said NO. I immediately felt horrible on the inside. So much so that after our talk had ended, I walked back up to him (in tears) and confessed that I did have a child. Her name was London. Sadly, she had passed away. It turned out the man was an elder at a nearby church, and he stopped exercising to pray over me right in the center of the gym. I made a vow to myself that day never to deny my child again. The mom in me couldn't forsake her existence, no matter how short-lived it was.

Surprisingly, the more I was asked this question the stronger I became. I eventually got to the point where I could talk about my daughter without having a meltdown. But deep down I was still hurting and knew I didn't want this to be the end of my motherhood story. Soon I made the decision to try to have another baby. I knew another child would never replace or erase the void and sorrow I had for London. My only hope was that having a new seed to grow, nurture and love would restore happiness to my life. But that seed seemed impossible to plant. After months of unsuccessful attempts to get pregnant, I finally went to see a fertility specialist. I underwent test after test after test. The results were all grim. I had fibroids lining the outside of my uterus, a gazillion polyps on the inside of my uterus, and both of my Fallopian tubes were completely blocked. I was told I couldn't get pregnant naturally and that my only option to bear a child was through IVF. There was only a 40% chance the IVF would work. However, my tests also revealed that I had a blood disorder which predisposed me to early miscarriage even if it were successful. One specialist told me if I were to get pregnant again there was a 60% chance I would lose the baby. In my mind I figured 40 plus 60 equaled a 100% likelihood I would never be able to conceive. But my yearning to have kids was so strong that I was willing to take my chances.

I was scared. Scared I'd lose another baby. Scared everything would happen all over again. I was still heavily grieving the loss of my daughter, but I somehow found the strength to push past my fears and continue along my journey to motherhood. I spent nearly a year going back and forth to the doctor. I started exercising three to four days a week and adopted a diet full of fertility-boosting foods I had read about on Google. I underwent multiple surgeries and had to inject myself with hormones several times a day, all to prepare my womb to receive my promised child. Only a handful of family and friends knew what I was doing. A few even questioned why I was putting myself through all this. But I wanted a baby more than anything in the world and was willing to go to extreme lengths to get one. After a few setbacks, I finally went through with the IVF transfer. My beautiful, precious embryos that had been waiting patiently on ice were placed inside my uterus in hopes they would continue the life that had already begun inside them. Never in my life had I been more nervous than the next two weeks that followed while I waited to learn if I were pregnant. I prayed incessantly. I would even go to the cemetery and pray over my daughter's grave. I promised her she would one day be a big sister. When I got the long-awaited call from my doctor, I could barely hold the phone for my hands shaking so much. Was she about to validate the symptoms I had already begun to experience? The nausea, back pains, sore boobs…was life growing inside of me? A few seconds into our call my heart stopped. My biggest fear had come true. My pregnancy did not sustain. I had suffered another loss. My doctor was so optimistic the IVF would work, but I had once again lost my battle with infertility.

As a mother grieving the loss of a child and desperately trying to have another to no avail, I was overwhelmed with feelings of sadness, hopelessness, and anger. I felt everyone around me was "living the life" while I was silently suffering. As I struggled navigating life amid this storm, at times I couldn't find the strength to keep pushing forward. But I knew what my end goal was and didn't want to give up. I had to find a way to pick myself up. I couldn't allow myself to drown in my sorrows. As much as I wanted to sit, cry, and compare my life to everyone else, this wouldn't bring about the joy and happiness I ultimately wanted. I had to gain control of my life. I had to stop and **B-R-E-A-T-H-E.**

"BREATHE-ing" is the seven actions I took to overcome my emotional war with infertility and grief. It helped me re-direct my thoughts and energy and was truly a lifesaver. Here's the breakdown:

BREATHE – B

Believe in miracles. In order to attain anything, I had asked God for, I had to first and foremost believe it was possible for me to be blessed. Throughout the years I had adopted the mindset that nothing good ever happens to me. My whole life had been full of struggle and rejection, and I honestly didn't believe I could truly have the desires of my heart. There's a line in the song *Two Wrongs* by Wyclef Jean and Claudette Ortiz – "I'm so used to the rain that I can't see the sunshine no more" – that describes exactly how I felt about myself and my reality. I didn't feel I was able of being blessed. Even as I stood in the middle of the NICU that fateful night watching doctors and nurses try to resuscitate my child I kept yelling out, *"God don't love me! God don't love me!"* But I had to make a change. The more I claimed sadness and depression, the sadder and more depressed I became. The more I told myself I'll never have a baby, the more difficult it was for my body to produce a seed. I had to shift my mindset. Though I had suffered miscarriages and child loss due to my body's inability to sustain a pregnancy, though the doctors had told me I was physically unable to conceive a child, I had to believe that somewhere, somehow a miracle lay in store for me that would bring forth the baby I so desperately wanted. I started speaking life into my womb. I started speaking to my unborn child. For it was only after I began to shift my thoughts and my energy that a different outcome could begin to manifest.

BREATHE – R

Remember it's not your fault. This is what I had to keep telling myself over and over and over. After losing my daughter, I spent so many days sitting in bed recalling every moment of my pregnancy, trying to figure out what I did wrong. Did I eat something that harmed my baby? Was I not drinking enough water? Was I on my feet too much? All these thoughts and more plagued my mind constantly. But I realized this was not healthy. I had to stop blaming myself. I had to stop analyzing every single action and every single bad choice I'd made over the course of my life and declaring it the reason why I was "being punished." There was nothing I did to cause my baby's demise. My battle with getting pregnant wasn't the result of me being cursed. Everyone faces struggle at some point during their life. Infertility was mine. Again, I had to shift my mindset. If I wanted a different outcome I had to stop blaming and start speaking blessings over my life.

BREATHE – E

Eliminate triggers. This was extremely crucial for me. At a point where I was extremely fragile, I had to avoid things that would cause me to have an emotional breakdown. For me, this included disconnecting from all social media. Although I'm always happy for any woman experiencing the joy of bringing new life into this world, seeing posts of birth announcements, and being flooded with baby pics were just too much for me to bear. It made me sad, it made me angry, and it sent my thoughts right back to that dark place I was working so hard to get away from. I also declined all invites to baby showers, children's parties, and any event geared toward children. I didn't want to have to put up a happy front for people, and I didn't want people to have to tiptoe around me to accommodate my feelings. My triggers were my responsibility. For the sake of my wellbeing, I had to remove myself from environments that weren't conducive to my emotional healing.

BREATHE - A

Allow time to heal. There's no timeline for grief. There's no end date for mourning. And that's not to say you should wallow in a sea of sadness forever, but you must move along at your own pace. My job tried to force me back to work before I was mentally and emotionally ready. People would tell me I needed to "move on." But I refused to allow anyone to rush my grief. Life had been forever changed for me. I couldn't just go back to the way things once were. I had a new normal. I was a childless mother. I had to prepare myself to navigate life with this new normal. So I took all the time I needed to heal from my loss and build myself up to where I felt stable enough to go back into the world. You don't just *move on* after losing a child. But with time and a healthy space to heal, you learn to *move forward*.

BREATHE - T

Talk it out. After losing my daughter my mind was in a state of emotional warfare. I did not know how to handle it in a healthy manner. Sure, I had certain family members and friends I could talk to, but I didn't want to overwhelm them with my sadness. I didn't want to be this constant cloud of depression that rained on their day. So I kept my feelings and emotions bottled up inside. Sometimes I would go for walks around my neighborhood and just cry. Crying was my only outlet. I didn't know what else to do. Without having something or someone around to lift me up, I was on the brink of a nervous breakdown. I started seeing a grief counselor, one of the best decisions I could have made. Therapy provided a safe space for me to express my deepest feelings without fear of being judged. It gave me a moment to let down my "*I'm fine*" exterior and be weak. But it also taught me how to redirect my thoughts and channel my energy into more positive efforts. This played a major role in my emotional healing.

BREATHE – H

Hit pause. I had to take a time-out to focus on me. This meant stepping away from my usual routine of taking care of everyone else and put that same time and energy into taking care of myself. I let go of a lot of commitments that took from me more than they gave to me. I became selfish with my time. Self-care became my Number One priority. In order to heal, I had to put me first.

BREATHE – E

Expect bad days, but do not feel bad about the good days. It goes without saying that grief brings about a lot of sad and emotionally draining days. You get so used to the sadness and depression that it becomes a part of your new normal, everyday life. When the day comes where you catch yourself finally smiling or find that the tears have stopped flowing, embrace it. For far too long I felt guilty for feeling happy. I associated my sadness with me honoring the memory of my daughter. If I went too long without crying or went too many days without visiting her grave, I shamed myself for "forgetting" about her. In time I realized that wasn't the case. I hadn't forgotten about my baby.... I was finally healing. I had started to BREATHE again.

The more I started to breathe, the more I opened myself up to blessings and possibilities. Now, I'm on a new survival journey...raising twins!

"Life doesn't come
with a manual;
it comes with a mother."

– Unknown

 Master Coach, Blogger, Author, Speaker, Trainer and #CEOMomma, Tamara C. Gooch is the Founder and CEO of Pink Pearl, LLC, a transformational movement that magnifies the triumphant voices and stories of women with boldness, confidence, and truth.

With PheMOMenon At Forty blog & The Savvy Entrepreneurs Incubator group, a think-tank, next-level innovative learning platform, Tamara has established the concept of online community building and engagement, building and creating an elite, high-result society of everyday women who are impacting the world in monumental ways. Her formula for success is simple – Faith, Fierceness, Fearlessness, Fabulousness, Action, and incessant Education.

Tamara propels her clients forward with the blueprint and tools needed to launch and grow a successful business and monetize their genius in the most efficient way, while enjoying their lives, time with family, and a lifestyle of freedom

PHEMOMENON AT FORTY

TAMARA C. GOOCH

\fi-mäm-ə-non
A unique woman whose goal as a mother is to be present, not perfect.

How many times as moms we've thought to ourselves, *I wish there were a manual to this thing called MOM life!* Why? Because being a mom is challenging at times and what works for one mom may not work for another mom.

I was fortunate enough to get the foundational wisdom from my mother. Yet she could not foresee what would happen in my life as a mother compared to how life was when she was a mother and a wife.

There are many things I've endured as a mother, especially a mother at the age of 19—that I truly wasn't ready for—so let me take you back to that year, Spring 1994.

I was a young 18-year-old who thought she was in love, not realizing it was only lust. However, a high school dropout who had made more than one wrong choice about her life and up to this point found herself approaching the age of 19 and pregnant.

What do you do when you're faced with a decision that you never saw coming? You see, I was the youngest of seven children, remarkably close to my parents and I was nervous to share the fact that I could possibly be pregnant. How was I going to tell my mother that her baby was about to have a baby? I was a young hothead living the life, or so I thought.

There were many thoughts that raced through my mind at that moment, I bought and took a home pregnancy test. *I dropped out of school in the 11th grade, I don't have a high school diploma, I'm working at a sub shop, not married, no savings— how am I going to do this if I am pregnant? I* kept asking myself questions. *Will he and I stay together? How am I going to break this to my parents? Oh no, my dad is going to be disappointed!*

As I stood there taking in a deep breath, I proceeded to take the pregnancy test. Patiently waiting, I started to see the results and I instantly cried. I knew at that moment when I got home that night, I would have to share with my mother that I needed to make an appointment to go see our primary care physician.

However, the funniest thing happened that night. As I sat in our den watching my favorite show, I took a long, deep breath and I called out for my mother to let her know that I had something to ask her. As she walked from the kitchen into the den, I could literally see my heart beating through my shirt. I didn't know how she was going to take this. I didn't know if she was going to yell, although my mother was not a woman who yelled a lot. I was afraid.

As I exhaled that deep, long breath and I turned to my left, I saw my mother standing there drying a dish. I said to her "Mom, I think we may need to call the doctor's office tomorrow because I need to go and see her." My mother slightly tilted her head and said to me, "Why, because you're pregnant?" At that moment, my heart dropped to my feet!

Well, being the youngest of seven children, we had family that was coming in that weekend. By the time my family from Louisiana showed up this was a family affair. The day of my appointment my family from out of town had been there for about a day and my mother had her pep talk with me, letting me know how disappointed she was at my actions, not at the blessing that was to come. You see in my family both of my parents were Christians; they didn't believe in anything other than that child being a blessing. So inside of that car sat me, my mother, my third-oldest sister, my sister-in-law, who is married to my third-oldest brother, and my other sister-in-law who is married to my fourth oldest brother. We headed over to the doctor's office, as nervous as I was, shaking like Don Knotts. I had already known what the results were going to be. But you know how that saying goes: The blood never lies!

The good thing about my doctor's office is that there's a lab right there so everything was sent over that day. We sat, we talked, we laughed, we cracked jokes, we talked seriously, and I got more pep talks. All the things a young woman would want and feel that she needs while waiting on something that is going to shock her family. But it wasn't going to shock her because she had already known that she was with child.

As the doctor returned after an hour, she excitedly said, "Congratulations you're pregnant!" They began to make the appointments for me for the other test to let us know how far along I was and for me to understand what was about to happen. As soon as we walked out of the doctor's office I threw up. Everyone began to laugh and say, "Yep, she's pregnant, there's that morning sickness."

This was a frustrating, yet exciting and happy moment because now my mother knew that I was pregnant. However, we needed to go home and tell my father that I was pregnant and then I had to break the news to the father. Well, the news went over well with my dad; he hugged me and let me know that he was disappointed in my actions, but that the blessing that I was carrying wasn't the sin. As beautiful as that was to hear, I still felt bad because I felt as though I let my parents down.

Now was the moment that I had to choose how I was going to tell the guy that I was dating at the time that he was about to be a father. *So how do you navigate through this?* I was asking myself. Well, the day came for us to sit down and talk. His family was everywhere in the house, and there was not one moment for us to have a private conversation.

I immediately seized an opportunity to go ahead and let him know that I was pregnant. The worst things flowed from his mouth at that moment and let me know that I would soon be raising this child on my own. Time went on, and I made decisions I knew I needed to make to have the life that I knew I deserved, not just for me but for the little one that I was carrying.

Being a high school dropout, not having my high school diploma or a GED at that moment and having to get on government assistance because I could not work due to bad morning sickness, afternoon, and evening sickness, I knew I needed to decide, quickly. My parents chose to tell me to stay at home for as long as I needed to take care of the baby. Once I got home, I lay in my bed that night and I took out my journal and I made my list of everything I knew I needed to do.

Fast forward, throughout the entire pregnancy everything was going well; the only downfall was the child's father never went to any appointments. His excuse was he had to work. However, my parents taught me that if that man can get you pregnant that man should be well enough or willing to help you take care of that child. Well, this proved to be so not true!

I kept a positive attitude throughout my entire pregnancy. I refused to let him or anyone else bring me down. I enrolled in a school for pregnant moms and was able to complete my high school diploma. My daughter was due Spring of 1994, and graduation was that June. I had made my mind up that I didn't want to walk the stage because I didn't want to leave my baby. However, I changed my mind and walked the stage anyway, with her in my arms.

Learning how to navigate my life as a 19-year-old mother with a newborn baby—what did that mean? That meant I needed a job, money, and peace of mind. But being a mother, a girlfriend, I also had to figure out what I was going to do with the rest of my life because now it wasn't just me; I had a little person who was looking up to me to take care of her.

For the next six years her father and I continued to parent. We had ups, we had downs and roller coaster rides—that relationship was so toxic that I didn't pay attention to any signs. I told myself I never wanted to be a statistic, so I would endure the verbal, mental, psychological, and on one or two occasions physical abuse. But as crazy as it sounded, I thought I was so much in love and I didn't want to be a statistic or a single mom or not married to the man that I had a child with. I decided we should just get married. So that's what we did.

This was one of the most makeshift courtroom marriages anyone could come up with. I ended up buying my own ring. My family and his family made sure that we had a great reception. Deep down in my heart I knew this marriage was not going to last, but something in me kept telling me to push through, don't give up, don't punk out, give it a try, maybe he'll change. Well, being married for one year and experiencing the things that I did took a toll on me. Motherhood brings about a change in a woman, if she's ready for it, that most don't see. Being a mother meant me becoming this lioness: I would protect my cub by any means. That meant protecting her from hearing abusive language, protecting her from seeing abusive actions—things that I never thought I would deal with, go through, or ever experience. I never thought that would be my life as a mother.

The moment things changed for me was that final night I lay in my bed and my seven-year-old little girl came in because she heard me cry. She crawled into bed with me, wiped my face and told me, "Mommy, we're going to be OK."

I knew at that moment something needed to change. See, there was the saying that my dad always told me: "Little boys playhouse, real men build homes." I had to come to terms with the fact that I was married to a little boy and that I was not going to let this little boy hurt me or my daughter ever again. I had to come to terms with the fact that I would soon become a single mom.

Wow, single mom! How does that sound—single mom?

The process to go through a divorce was easy but now I had to figure out how I would navigate my life now that I was about to be a single mother. This was a faith move. That's all I could think it would have been. I was me being bold and brave enough. My mother and I drove around a neighborhood and we looked at houses for rent.

I didn't have all of the money I needed in order to rent my own place, but as I stood there and I talked to the landlord and I explained to him my situation, I let him know that this abusive marriage would be over soon but that I needed a place to call my own. I asked him if he would be willing to hold that apartment for $300. He looked at me, he looked at my mother, he saw the sincerity, and he said, "No need in giving me that $300. I have two more weeks to bring the apartment up to where I want it to be and I'll get you the key and the leasing agreement and you can move in within the next three weeks."

Well, that's all I needed to know. You see, no matter the fear I felt, no matter the anger I felt, no matter the hurt I felt, no matter the anxiousness, or the doubt, I knew I needed to leave.

So for the next 15-plus years I would navigate the waters of being a single mother. That meant my life had to change. Things that I used to do I couldn't do anymore; places I used to go I couldn't go any longer. Why? Because I had responsibility!

Responsibility meant I needed to make sure our future was safe. I needed to make sure that I had food on the table. I needed to make sure that I had the kind of job that allowed me to take care of my household, my daughter, myself, and save for the future. For her future!

The harsh reality was that I was a single mom for 15 years. Any storm you can imagine going through, I experienced. I was that woman who decided that my daughter was more important than my dating. Although I did date, no men ever saw the inside of my home. One thing I knew was that I was not going to be that woman who had a revolving door when it came to men. I just knew that I never wanted to be that kind of mother or that kind of woman.

Those years went by because I made a conscious decision and I was going to stick with it. My daughter was to me the perfect little angel. She hardly ever got into any trouble in school, and if she did, it was for what most kids got in trouble for, talking. But she was a stellar student, a great child. She kept me busy and on my toes. I remained active, not just in her school, but making the decision to go back to school for me.

Then came the moment that I was introduced to a young man who was at the church where I was considering becoming a new member. Now my daughter was approaching her last year of high school, preparing to go off to college. How God orchestrated some things I will never under-stand. After 15 years of being a single mother and going through hell and back, I met someone, and we hit it off. Not understanding who he was or how he was, my daughter took to him.

I didn't realize that my daughter and his son were very close and acted as if they were naturally brother and sister. He and I began working together in the church on every financial project and ministry team there was. We worked so well together during our time we became best friends and got to know each other well. We both knew that we were divorced, single parents, so he saw the opportunity to ask me out after some time. Making that decision to ask me out on a date led us to dating for about seven months and him asking my father for my hand in marriage. This all took place in 2011. By the end of 2011 we had made the decision to be married March 2012. A year and a half later, I became pregnant!

Instead of me being an empty nester and prepping myself to go on a cruise while my daughter went off to college, I was prepping myself to be a 39-year-old with child. I had sunk into a deep depression because I never wanted another child and I knew I would be 40 giving birth. But the blessing in all of this was knowing that I was carrying a little person that would be a blessing to my husband.

The storms that we weathered this time were slightly different because I didn't have to weather these storms alone. I had someone to go through the storms with me.

One thing we know about mothers is that we do a lot. We work, we cook, we stay home with the kids, we plan play dates, we drop kids off at school, we clean, we do laundry, we create lists, we check items off the list, we change diapers, we change sheets after accidents, we grocery shop, we plan, we build up our husbands, we tend to our marriages and friendships, we treat ourselves sometimes to a manicure and maybe a pedicure.

The point is, we get things done. As someone who spent 15 years as a single mother, there was a lot that fell on my shoulders, but the husband that I have now asked me one question that I completely fell apart on: "With you taking care of everyone else, when was the last time someone took care of you?"

You see, I believe that we do what we do by the grace of God, and we all know that God gives us the passion and perseverance in motherhood, which requires mental strength to keep trying day after day, no matter how many times we get knocked out, because boy oh boy, we do get knocked down. Not only do we deal with all the things that I mentioned previously, we're giving birth to children and dealing with postpartum depression and anxiety while still being required to show up when others aren't feeling well or even when we aren't feeling well.

Yet through everything that I mentioned, everything that I endured, the various forms of abuse, deciding to divorce, deciding that I was not going to allow my daughter to see abuse, giving birth not once but twice—for every mom reading this right now, I want you to understand something more about who we are as strong women, as strong mothers. I titled this PheMOMenon At Forty because we are moms who are phenomenal; we have the humility and the wherewithal to know when things aren't going the way they should. Some of us have the innate ability to ask for help when needed. We put our children before our own desires, we focus on physical and emotional health to lend to our children and to others, and we play an active role in helping others in our community. Some of us have the ability to set limits and some of us don't. We share our life lessons with our children, whether they listen or not. Many of us are becoming more and more honest with our own struggles. We choose to make choices that suit our households, and as you know that old saying goes, "Mom knows best" because we do. So whatever it is that you may be going through, you are a phenomenal mother and God created you for a greater purpose.

A MOM is all those things previously mentioned and more because we can guide our children through the darkest caves. Why? Because we've lived in some of the darkest moments. We are like the pearl; that irritant gets inside of us; that postpartum depression or anxiety, that child with autism, that child that's been bullied or the child who is the bully; that child who's incarcerated or that child who becomes pregnant at a young age. A divorce, annulment, abuse—so many other things that moms must deal with and go through. But because we know how to weather that storm, put on that brave face, and eventually face that storm head-on, we're able to guide our children through the dark caves and over the highest mountains. Some of us are bold enough to speak to those mountains and tell those mountains to move because they're not going to mess with our cub. Mom, I want you to know that you are a pheMOMenon, whether you are 30, 40 or 50, and know that you are never alone.

Erica Anderson is a licensed and ordained elder, certified Christian life coach, and special education administrator. She is the CEO of Erica Anderson Ministries and can often be found delivering a "Cup of Encouragement" on Facebook Live. She has an Ed. S. degree in Educational Leadership from Berry College, a Master's Degree in Special Education from the University of Phoenix and a Batchelor of Arts Degree from the University of Georgia.

Erica is passionate about intercessory prayer and seeing women healed, set free and delivered. She has dedicated her life to using her gifts and talents to be a blessing to others. She enjoys, skating, hiking, bike riding and special time making memories with her family. In her coaching, mentoring and ministry endeavors, she seeks to bring out the best in others while helping them to see and reach their fullest potential.

Erica is a wife and mother of a son and a daughter and is also a grandmother. She resides in Newnan, Georgia with her husband and daughter.

14 YEARS AND 1 DAY
PARENTING IN THE GAP

ERICA ANDERSON

Motherhood for me was one of the most edifying yet paralyzing, terrifying, and rewarding experiences in my life. The edifying emotion came from the fact that I had been chosen to bring another life into the world. Paralyzed is what I felt when I first heard the news from the doctor. I was terrified because I questioned my ability to parent with no experience with siblings or babies. The rewarding moments of motherhood continue to unfold in front of my eyes as I have watched the two amazing humans that I birthed evolve into a teenager and a man with his own family.

The institution of motherhood stretched me beyond measure. I was stretched physically, emotionally, psychologically, spiritually, and even literally as I found myself trying to figure out how I was going to steward that which God had entrusted me with. Questions and fears became woven into my fabric as I contemplated this bigger than life undertaking. Can I do this? Will I be successful? Will I fail? How will my life change? What have I done? Am I ready for this? What will people think? This line of questioning quickly became a part of the interrogation process that I engaged in. Your mind becomes endlessly bombarded as you ponder this journey into the unknown. Even though many have traveled this road, there is nothing to adequately prepare you when it's your turn. Every mother experiences motherhood in her own unique way and no two motherhood experiences are alike.

Even though there are countless books written about motherhood and parenting, nothing can adequately prepare you for this experience except for the experience itself. I read books about what to expect during pregnancy, tips for first-time mothers, changes your body will experience, books about the most popular baby names, and others. What I did not find in my search was a book about how to parent in the gap and raise two kids with a fourteen-year age difference.

Allow me to take you on my journey of parenting in the gap. A gap represents an unfilled space or a break in continuity. Certainly, fourteen years represents a definite unfilled space and break in continuity. Siblings that are close in age provide shared and similar experiences. There is an opportunity for common ground.

Parenting in the gap for me encompassed various phases and challenged my abilities to multitask in ways that seemed at times impossible. I am the proud mother of a son and a daughter who were born 14 years and 1 day apart. Who knew that conception for me would happen twice around the same time and delivery would occur on almost the same date? As my due date for my daughter approached, I prayed earnestly for them not to be born on the same day. It was okay for them to share me, but I did not want them to share the same birthday. That, to me, would have been disastrous.

God knew the plan before the beginning of time, just as He knew that you would be reading this book at this time. We think we have a plan, but His plans and thoughts are always higher and better than ours. Parenting has its own set of unique challenges; however, parenting in the gap transcends anything that you can imagine. There really are no designated hard and fast rules as it relates to the ideal age difference between siblings. There are those who suggest that siblings should be a couple of years apart, while others attest that five years is better because it gives the mother the opportunity to share the excitement with the oldest child. When God decides to bring a child to this earth He does not consult with medical science or the Internet when He decides to bestow the honor of motherhood upon us. For that, I am grateful.

As an only child my upbringing was one where I was surrounded with friends and cousins but no siblings. My parents were my first playmates and I spent most of my time with my father playing catch, shooting hoops, and basically going with him everywhere he went. My mother introduced me to fine dining and the best shopping excursions a girl could ask for and all things fancy. The only child experience was one replete with days of learning how to entertain myself and rare opportunities of having to share with anyone else.

I never really gave much intense thought to having children because "only children" can often become self-absorbed and very much in their own world. I was comfortable with solitude, independent, confident, could entertain myself and acted more like an adult because I was mainly exposed to adult conversations. Adversely, there were times when I lacked diplomacy, had a "my way or the highway" mentality, and could be emotionally needy. Because my children were born in what I perceive to be two worlds apart, their lives closely mimicked that of two siblings that were raised as only children. I knew the life of an only child but found it difficult at times to parent two only children who were also siblings.

My journey to motherhood began when I had my first child at the age of 29. I learned that I was pregnant after having been married for one month. There was a myriad of emotions that ran through my head. Initially I was overwhelmed by a blend of hormonal and emotional changes while learning how to be a wife. My pregnancy was unremarkable in that I experienced little to no complications and did not look pregnant until I was about six months.

Once my son was born, I felt deluged with emotions and full of uncertainty. I wondered how I would parent this tiny human full of potential and limitless possibilities. He was totally dependent on me as his mother, regardless of how inept I thought I was at the moment. Again, the questions began to invade my headspace. How was I going to effectively navigate the terrain of mothering? How would I provide the foundation conducive for his happiness, success, and ultimate confidence? Did I have what it takes to guide him to the highest version of himself?

The answers to these questions did not come easy. At best, I could only resolve to do the best I could with what I had, realize that "supermom" is not a real person, and come to the realization that since God had called me to this challenge I was already equipped and up to the task. Only God can give the gift of life and when He gives life the plans for that life have already been established. Our job as mothers is to properly steward the gifts of life God has given us.

The perfectionist in me wanted to do everything right. I wanted him to have the perfect formula, the perfect clothing, the perfect environment, the perfect daycare and ultimately the perfect life. How was I going to be perfect at something that I had never experienced? Perfection does not belong in the repertoire of a mother.

My son was born during a season when the Atlanta Braves were in the playoffs and there was much excitement surrounding his birth. The moment our eyes met, I knew that God had equipped me with everything I needed and more to mother this precious gift.

During the first eight months of my son's life I had the opportunity to stay at home with him and this time gave us the opportunity to bond. We spent our days playing, laughing, and bonding as only a mother and son can. One day this time of happiness and bonding quickly shifted into something unimaginable. Shortly before my son's second birthday, he and my husband were involved in a horrific car accident which left me functioning as a single parent and my husband in a coma and incapacitated.

At this point motherhood took on another meaning as I traversed very difficult waters which caused me to believe that I would drown miserably. Again, the questions came back with a vengeance. *How do I handle this by myself? What does this look like long term? How am I going to be able to manage raising a toddler and caring for a husband who is in a coma and incapacitated? Is being a good mother by myself going to be good enough?* My marriage ultimately dissolved, and single parenting became a stark reality for me.

During this time, I worked tirelessly to remain gainfully employed, ensured that food was on the table, and managed a household while remaining emotionally and physically present for my son. Motherhood during this season was very enigmatic and unclear. The motherhood lines were blurred, to say the least. The view that was once clear became cloudy and uncertain. My twenty-four-hour days seemed as if they lasted forever and there was never enough time to get everything accomplished.

Every hour, every minute, and every second of my life seemed divided into a million places. Time spent on any one task left me torn and wondering if I should be doing something else. As my son grew, I quickly realized that boys are rambunctious, active, loud, energetic, and physically aggressive! I learned some valuable tips along the way, which included monitoring aggression, modeling good behavior, looking beyond the dirt and the noise, and various ways to clean white baseball pants soiled with red dirt!

Later came the innumerable hours of sports, the games, the practices, the late-night activities on school nights, team mom duties and countless play dates with other boys, which included roughhousing that carried on for what seemed like hours. While engaging in these activities I felt comfortable because my energy level was still pretty high and most of the other mothers were my age. We were all in this together, so I did not feel out of place. During this time, because of my age, I had the energy level and the tenacity to keep up with all the activities that were associated with raising a boy, or so I thought.

Raising a boy as a single parent in my late twenties had its share of challenges. I knew that I could not teach him how to be a man, but I tried to surround him with role models and others who could share some very poignant lessons and advice with him that I could not. When my son turned fourteen motherhood took on yet another dynamic because I remarried. This turn of events revealed yet another layer of my motherhood adventure.

At the age of 14 boys, whether intentionally or unintentionally, assume the role of man of the house in the absence of a father figure. It often becomes difficult to co-parent when a child has been accustomed to having you to themselves exclusively. Needless to say, the plot thickened. Just when I thought things could not get any more interesting, they did. I remarried; the same year I was remarried we discovered that I was pregnant at the age of forty-three.

The endless questions began to bombard me again. This time they came with a vengeance. This set of questions drove deeper into my thought pattern and were on an entirely different level. I was not necessarily concerned about what do to this time. *How hard could it be to be a mother again? I've done it before; surely I can do it again, right?* My concerns this time were centered around how to do this at forty-three as opposed to twenty-nine. Not only was there going to be a gap between the ages of my children; there was a huge gap between where I was mentally, physically, and emotionally. Age was just another consideration. *Am I going to be able to carry this child full-term? Are there going to be any chromosomal abnormalities associated with this pregnancy due to my age? Will I survive childbirth? How expensive is childcare these days? How will I manage this with my husband and me living in different states? What will this mean to the child we already had? How is he going to be impacted.? How is he going to feel about sharing me with my husband and now a new baby? How will the family dynamics change? What are people going to think since I am 43?*

As you can tell, this time around there were a lot more concerns and considerations to be addressed. Getting pregnant at forty-three took a little getting used to. Initially I did not tell anyone because I did not know how the news was going to be received and I was trying to get accustomed to it myself. Once the news had been shared, I began to settle in with the idea that I had become chosen to be someone's mother again and I embraced the will of God for my life.

This pregnancy was not unlike my first. I did not have complications but did have some reservations when I was told by my physician that I fell into the high-risk category due to my age. There were several tests that were suggested to determine if there were any abnormalities. We decided against them because the outcome was not going to impact our choice to welcome this wonderful blessing into the world and into our lives and family.

During this time in my life, exhaustion was an understatement as a descriptor of how I felt from day to day. The mix between a middle schooler with raging hormones and a baby requiring feedings and diaper changes was more than a notion. Sleep deprivation was at an all-time high and it was commonplace for me to change my sleep pattern to accommodate the needs of the children.

Being pregnant while raising a fourteen-year old brought its own set of unique and interesting challenges. I was no longer able to comfortably sit on the hard, wooden benches at the baseball field. There were many days when my "get up and go" got up and went.

My husband and I were in a long-distance marriage for the first seven months of pregnancy. Shortly before the birth of our daughter, my husband moved from out of state and we began preparing for our little bundle of joy.

Mothering children at different ages requires a mother to realize that her children have different needs based on their age and in order to facilitate positive growth and development, it is necessary to discern which child needs what and when. The transition to a second child was a very different experience for me than it was for many that I knew because of the age difference. At times it felt like I was a part of two different families with the responsibility of molding the two together as one. In the middle of the chaotic moments of diaper changing and futile attempts at breastfeeding, I was helping my son with science projects and taking him to male bonding "play" dates with friends. My life appeared to be the consummate constant juggling act between mixing baby formula and making preparations for the eighth-grade dance.

It was at this time that I realized the true extent of the impact of parenting in the gap. The reality set in and weighed like a ton of bricks. Time and energy spent time with one child left me feeling as though I needed to be with the other. The emotional and physical demands of parenting in the gap left me feeling like I was never fully present for each child, as I attempted to attend to and care for siblings with what seemed like diametrically opposed needs.

I began to notice that even though my children were siblings they had very little in common due to their age difference, except for the fact they shared me as their mother. There are very few things that a teenager and a newborn can enjoy together. As a mother one of my greatest desires was for them to grow up together in closeness as I had observed in other siblings. What I failed to take into consideration was that most siblings I had witnessed were much less than fourteen years apart in age, which made it easier for them to connect.

When parenting in the gap, as a mother, I had to abandon my ideal of what I thought my children's relationship should be and accept it as it was. Perhaps I projected my sibling relationship desires upon my own children based on what I wished for myself as an only child. Instead of placing emphasis on the relationship between the two I began to embrace the changes that occurred within me as I parented in the gap.

While parenting in my late twenties and early thirties I felt equipped to deal with the stress of pregnancy and parenting. I had somewhat of a cohort of associates and friends that I could share the experience with and discuss resources. In my thirties I'd had enough life experiences and my career path was somewhat established.

Parenting in my forties gave me the benefit of perspective that made me patient and calm. Situations which would ordinarily rattle me as a mother did not have the same impact. I have become resigned to the fact that motherhood has provided a number of interesting nuances such as pain, joy, frustration, patience, stress, and happiness. If I had not experienced motherhood again at forty-three, I probably wouldn't have a clue what TikTok was or know what it's like for your child to call you "bro."

Nevertheless, this is the journey that I have been destined to take and I am excited about continuing to enjoy the ride. There will be curves, and bumps, detours, and some stalls along the way, but I can assure you that you are made for this. I am now the proud mother of a 27-year old and a 13-year old whom I love to the moon and back.

Nadian Reid is a certified Christian Life Coach and Newborn Care Specialist. She is a Psychology and Theology Student at Grace Christian University. Nadian is the CEO/Founder/Owner of SuperMothers Strength Int'l which carries the mission to inspire mothers of all races, cultures, and nationalities to seek, find and fulfil their God given purpose as mothers.

Nadian is also the founder of Lady Theresa's Foundation. She is a philanthropist at heart whose life mission is to assist and relieve broken, helpless, Mothers through social, spiritual, and financial support. She is a God-fearing single mother's advocate who uses her story as a broken teen mom to inspire mothers. A powerful and anointed speaker, she is dubbed the "Prolific Transformational Preacher." She is a lover of children and a student of the word.

COPARENTING WITH OUR ETERNAL FATHER

THERESA NADIAN REID

"Casting all your care upon him; for he careth for you." 1 Peter 5:7
(KJV)

As I hurried to the bus stop with my one-week-old baby on one shoulder and his diaper bag on the other, I was unsure about what I was doing. The feeling of insecurity crowded my mind and I wished I had someone by my side to relieve me of my anxieties, help ease the burdens and reassure me that all would be well. I had always tried to maintain a positive mindset during my pregnancy despite the insensitive things that were said about me, compounded by my own insecurities as a teen mom. I was the hot topic on the lips of my then church brethren and neighbors. I was unmarried and pregnant and to make matters worse, I was a teenager. I felt broken, lonely, and afraid but I was optimistic about my future. I never entertained the thoughts that life for me was over. Unaware of a mother's role, I was worried and fearful of making mistakes that could be detrimental to both my young child and myself. I was immature and very naïve, but I knew life happened and I had to take responsibility for my actions.

My body was still sore from the pain and agony I endured while laboring to bring forth a promise. I was extremely tired and drained and needed both emotional and physical support. To my surprise I saw my son's dad on my way to the hospital, and I released a sigh of relief. I thought he had come to my rescue and would be delighted to assist me and so I asked him if he could accompany me to the hospital to get the baby's eyes checked for what I thought was an infection. He stared in my eyes and told me, "No." As far as I was aware there was no valid reason for his refusal to assist, and he didn't seem obliged to provide one.

I could not recall ever feeling so ashamed. I felt immensely rejected. This was not the first time he had denied me assistance or support, but this time, I was crushed because I was tired and desperate for his support. My body felt numb and I began to shake. With tears streaming down my face, I pressed my way to the bus stop, but my speed declined as I felt heavy, like an elephant was on my back weighing me down. I could barely walk. I felt forsaken in a time when I needed someone, especially the person who should have been there for me and our baby the most. With all the drama I had gone through during my period of gestation and now with this encounter, I felt like I was already on my journey to being a single mother, but I was fearful of facing motherhood alone and as puzzled as I was, I tried to justify his actions and gave him the benefit of the doubt, although it was the hardest thing to do.

Isaiah 41:10 "Fear thou not; for I am with thee: be not dismayed; for I am thy God; I will strengthen thee; yea, I will help thee..."

Mothers, there are days when you may have to walk your motherhood journey with no one physically present by your side. These times can be really hard and cause you to feel forsaken, fearful, and hopeless, especially if it is in a time when you are in need. But rest assured, God is with you always. He shows up and even speaks to us in different ways, but sometimes we cannot see or hear because our attention is fixed on how we think He should show up. But God's ways of doing things cannot be fathomed; His help is perfect. And according to Jeremiah 29:11, "...He knows the plans that He has for our lives..." therefore we need not worry. There are times when we feel as though we are walking *through* fire, or through deep waters. But note the word *"through"*—it means that there is an *"exit."* A pastor once said sometimes you have to go down to come up, but you always have to go *"through"* to come out.

The Bible tells us to put our entire trust in God and ask Him daily to lead, guide, direct, protect and provide for us. According to Psalms 118:8 (KJV), "It is better to trust in the Lord than to put confidence in man." Jesus will never fail you and all He wants is for you to acknowledge that you cannot be the mother you desire to be all by yourself and become vulnerable to Him. Remember that our children are a blessing from God, the fruit of our wombs which is His reward, and so we are co-parents with God. He owns these children but has given us stewardship of them. Therefore, He will take care of them; they are not bastards; they have a Father who loves, adores, and cherishes them—an eternal Father who will be with them until eternity.

An important thing to always bear in mind is that co-parenting with Him will lift the unnecessary burdens we often try to carry all by ourselves. He wants to care for His children in every way and especially in ways that we cannot.

I have been co-parenting with God for about fifteen years. It has not been easy because there are times when the human in me wants to be independent, but those were the times when I ended up doing the wrong things; they were many, but had it not been for the Father God, my child would be left fatherless. I would have thrown in the towel a long time ago because each day brings something new and I never know what to expect.

Affirmation: I am called by God to be a mother and He is the Father of my children. He is with me; He is in me and He is guiding me. I am strong and courageous because there is a MOM in me.

When I finally got on a bus, I sat there feeling lost, lonely, and confused. My thoughts were restless, as I was still consumed with the thought of my child's father refusing to accompany and assist me in seeking medical attention for the baby. The more I thought about it, the more my body became unresponsive to its senses. I felt numb and weak.

While seated on the bus, there was a young man next to me who was from my community. He rubbed his shoulder against mine and whispered jokingly, "Just pretend that I am the father." We both laughed. I don't know if he read my mind or knew of my situation, but his humor and words were appreciated. I heard he was a very humorous guy and you could not be around him and not laugh. That day was my first close encounter with him, and he certainly made me laugh despite my emotional trauma.

When we disembarked the bus, he said to me, "I can't let my baby's mother walk the rest of the journey to the hospital," so he chartered a ride for me. I could have walked the distance, as I had already made up my mind to do; however, the sun was extremely hot, as it was on any other day in Jamaica, and the walk was also lengthy.

After I arrived at the hospital, I was told by a nurse that I should have gone to the one nearest to my community and had no need to come to this one. However, I was told when discharged from the hospital after I had my son to return there in the case of an emergency. I was certain I had made the right choice. I tried to communicate that to the nurse but was refused assistance. With all that I had already encountered earlier that morning, I was mentally and emotionally drained and had no energy to argue the matter, so I followed the directives that were given without any objection. I was still in a state of shock and confusion. I headed to the hospital I was told to go to, which was closer to my home. After reaching there, I was sent back to the one where I had given birth and was just refused assistance with the explanation that my and my baby's records were there and that is where I should seek assistance. I explained what transpired when I visited earlier but was told that there was nothing they could do and that it was protocol. As frustrated as I was becoming, I tried to understand, and I left. The nurse also told me that I should not leave the hospital when I returned there until the baby was seen by a doctor.

Sad, lonely, sick, disappointed, hopeless and broken are just a few words to describe how I felt, but I had a responsibility to ensure that the baby God entrusted me with was in good health, hence no matter the obstacles I was not going to give up, and so I made my way yet again to the hospital I first visited that morning.

On my second trip to the hospital I sat on the bus and there was a lady looking at me. Her eyes were filled with care and compassion. I felt like I knew her, but I could not recall from where. We had a brief conversation and at the end of the journey on the bus, she offered to accompany me to the hospital. I was overwhelmed with joy, as I desperately needed the help. Deep within I knew she meant well. That morning she was heading to school, The University of the West Indies, and was late for class, but she did not mind helping me. In fact, she made it a part of her mission. She spent some time with me before leaving for school.

A few years after rededicating my life to the Lord, I met her at the church where I was a new candidate. That was her place of worship. The lady was like an angel; she was gentle, soft-spoken and had an excellent spirit and a bright smile on her face that made me feel reassured and safe. I am convinced that God used her that morning to rescue a broken, helpless, lonely teenage mother. I was overjoyed that our paths had collided yet again so that I could express thanks to her for coming to my rescue.

My baby was finally seen by a doctor although it was almost evening. The doctor reported that the mucus coming from his eyes was normal and was nothing to worry about.

On my way back home, I was in pain and had no idea how I was going to make it or what time I would get home. The evenings were usually busy and getting on a bus from the town to my community was extremely difficult. While walking to the bus stop, I heard someone calling out to me. I recognized the voice and so I looked back and saw that it was a gentleman who I usually purchased fruits from while attending antenatal clinic. He and his wife expressed how they were longing to see me but knew I'd had a baby and understood why they hadn't been seeing me. They were happy to see us and even offered to take us home because it was too late to travel alone. For the third time in one day, when I thought I was about to collapse, help came in the form of human agents.

Sometimes we have to be open to receive help. I do not mean that every help that comes our way is from God, but He certainly shows up when we are in dire need. I had no doubt that my help came from God that day as I prayed for it. It is of utmost importance to always pray and seek God's guidance because He will not allow the devil to destroy his children. I knew God was on my side and He was reassuring me that He would never leave nor forsake me.

I cannot recall praying that particular morning and asking God for this kind of help, but my prayers were always centered around, "God help me." He certainly "looked beyond my faults and saw my need."

I was oblivious of what it takes to raise a child. I had my mother, who was very helpful, but I felt ashamed to ask her for assistance when I needed it because she was still in a state of disappointment; therefore, I chose to always seek God's help and be open to receive it in whatever way He sent it.

He is a present help in times of trouble according to Psalms 46:1. He will never leave nor forsake us, as written in Psalms 27:10, and that is a promise He will keep until eternity.

On that day He sent just the help I needed and even more through three persons when I was looking for it from one man. God could have used one person to do it all, but I believe He was showing me that He is the God of abundance and He expressed His love for me and our son every step of the way through the hearts of others. I cannot tell you how I would have made it through that day had He not shown up.

Being just a teenager, I lacked knowledge about life and its lessons and was insensible to the potential menaces of proceeding with a relationship that seemed unfruitful. I was focused on giving my child what I knew every child needed, and that was having both parents together. I was willing to put behind me how the father consistently treated me and move forward. Also, that was my first relationship and my little heart thought it was in love.

Four months after having my son, I ventured into entrepreneurship. My products and services were in high demand and there were days when I had to trek miles to make deliveries. My mother objected because she ensured my baby and I were always taken care of, but I wanted to take responsibility for my actions and to become financially independent so I could finance myself and return to school. I thought I owed that to my parents. I always believed that I was destined for greatness and having a baby did not kill that aspiration. I had goals and they had to be achieved. After completing my final year in high school, which was put on hold due to my pregnancy, my small business was exhausted and needed to be replenished. Thankfully, I found employment.

There are times when you may feel like you have to give something up to get something, and while it is true, because the Bible tells us to give and we shall receive good measure, pressed down, shaken together, and running over, as seen in Luke 6:38, it is not so in all cases. As mothers, we tend to give up our happiness for the sake of our children and put on a mask to hide the pain and hurt, giving the impression that everything is well. We sacrifice our happiness so that they can be happy. May I submit to you that if you are not emotionally healthy, your children will not be healthy and thriving either. The home will be toxic and chaotic or whatever you are trying to hold on to for their sake can eventually destroy both you and your children. It is important for you to understand that you cannot give what you do not have. They need stability and security and so do you. As mothers it is highly possible that we may encounter challenging moments that can put our mental health at risk. I wish I had known this as a teenage mother, but it took my experiences to understand life like I do now.

The relationship with my son's dad, the one I was willing to sacrifice my happiness for, almost cost me my sanity. Promise after promise was broken. We both had our flaws and he had a girlfriend among other women prior to us getting together, but I was afraid to let go when I found out, which I thought was too late because I was already ripe with a child. His girlfriend was loved and accepted by his mother and I was resented and rejected. I used my vulnerability, naivety, insecurity, brokenness, and confused mind to blame myself for the mishaps in our relationship.

I cannot tell what was going through his mind when he promised me that he was leaving Jamaica to visit America for a short time but he would come back to marry me and join me on my walk of faith because he knew that was important to me. I was convinced and filled with joy. The world would finally see that he really loved me. Again, another promise was broken.

I did not know the date when he was leaving. He left without saying goodbye. I did not hear from him for a long time. Then, to my surprise, I got the news that he was married and had started a new family in the USA. I had a mental breakdown but tried to pretend all was well for the sake of my son, although my emotional illness could not be hidden.

By this time, I not only felt like I was a single mom, I knew it, and the reality was that this man had left me to take care of a child all by myself. I was in my early twenties and my son was about five. This time I had to move on. I didn't know how but I was intentional about it. That was when I learned to pray sincere prayers that moved the hands of God. By that time, I had to learn how to co-parent with God, knowing that He was my present and only help. I then learned that I needed to let go of my son's father emotionally (as he was already gone physically) and allow God to fill the gap.

There are stories in the Bible of single mothers but one that I found relatable and that really moved me was the story of Hagar. I could relate with her brokenness and her situation of being deserted and rejected by the father of her son. I can only imagine how sad, shattered, and distressed she must have felt, but God showed up on her behalf (Genesis 16:6-11). While our stories might have not been entirely the same there were some similarities in how we may have felt after being rejected by the father of our children, while their fathers moved on and continued their lives with their wives. I pressed my way to the altar in God's presence. My healing was slow but sure.

One Sunday after church it dawned heavily on me that I hadn't heard from my son's dad in almost a year. I was left alone without any help. I felt deserted. I had to help my toddler son to cope with the complete absence of his father and at this point I was tired of making excuses for him.

That night I reflected on the story of Paul and Silas's encounter with Jesus while they were locked up in prison. They cried out to him at midnight and he heard and set them free, according to Acts 16:25-26. I felt like I was locked up in a prison of pain, disappointment, rejection, financial distress, and being ridiculed for too long and so I decided to lift up my voice unto the Lord at midnight. My sister Tashina was with me and she was at her breaking point of seeing me struggling, and so she travailed with me that night. The Lord heard the cries of a desperate mother and with urgency He answered.

The following morning, I received a call from my son's dad. He had sent remittance. He could not even spare five minutes to find out how his firstborn was doing. After seeing how quickly God answered me, I started praying at midnight, especially when I needed a breakthrough. I developed a love for prayer because it gave me such peace of mind, strengthened my faith, and gave me reassurance that God cares, even if the prayers are not immediately answered.

I learned how to dedicate my child to the Lord on the altar each day and offer him as a sacrifice. The struggles were real, but I refused to throw in the towel. I was now getting used to co-parenting with God. He taught me how to cast all my cares on Him, to be a mother and not to assume the role of a father because He is.

Sometimes situations may cause you to come to a halt on your path to a better life, but it doesn't matter where you've stopped, you can make a fresh start. It is inevitable for a vehicle to get a flat tire, but that doesn't necessarily mean the journey should be discontinued. And so it is with single parenting: The struggles are inescapable, they will force you to give up, but if you place your hands in God's you will not be overcome.

No one else can travel this rocky road like you; however, God will provide help along the way. Sometimes it may even require you to go some extra miles that were not planned, but if getting to your destination means a lot to you then you will press your way to the finish line no matter what.

In Hebrews 12:2 it tells us that "…Jesus is the author and finisher of our faith; who for the joy that was set before Him endured the cross, despising the shame…"

I used prayer as my *GPS*. I call it my "Guiding Positioning System," and of course there are times when I misunderstand what God is saying and do the opposite. There are times when I tried to do things on my own, but I always ended up back in the presence of the Lord because only He has the answer.

You may be in a deserted place like Hagar, abandoned and rejected by the father of your children and wondering how you are going to do this on your own. Or maybe you are experiencing lack like the widow who had just a day's meal for her and her son. Perchance you could even be suffering a loss like Naomi. Whether it's your job, home, marriage, business or just about anything that rendered you a single mom, I want you to know that God cares. Before He placed that seed inside your womb, He knew that child and had ordained him to be great. Do not feel bitter; God will make your life even better than it was before you became a single mom. And it will be the best if you co-parent with Him. "You can do all things through Christ which strengthens you," according to Philippians 4:13.

I encourage you, no matter what happens, do not give up on your children. Their earthly fathers may not be there to give them the support that they need, but you are. Love them without limitations, pray for them daily, encourage and support them. Do not belittle them or make them feel unworthy. Call them by their names, tell them that they are the best gift you've ever had and make them feel like the blessing they truly are. I know that the possibility of getting frustrated at times is real, but avoid comparing them with their fathers, even if it's a positive attribute. This can cause them to start asking questions about their dads that you may not be prepared to answer. They are not failures; their dads failed, and they will succeed in all their endeavors. They were made in the likeness and image of God their Father. Ask God to make them over each day to represent Him (Genesis 1:27, KJV). God trusts you to be their mother; don't fail them by trying to do what only GOD can do. You may be a "single mother" but you don't have to remain that way. Co-parent with HIM today and you will begin to enjoy the peace, joy and love that's wrapped up in these beautiful gifts from God that were sent to you on the day you gave birth to that promise.

As you travel this path of uncertainty, be reminded that God will never leave you. It is a mother's choice to remain a single mother because God is a Father to the Fatherless according to Psalms 68:5. And He is ready and willing to co-parent with you.

Affirmation: I am not afraid of the unknown because GREATER is He in me, and that makes me a SuperMother. My strength comes from the Supreme Being. There is a GREATER MOM in me!

Mia Turner-Whitley has co-authored two anthologies, "No Glory Without A Story" and "Phenomenal Woman: Still Standing". She is the CEO of MIASpeaks. She provides vision webinars, keynote speaking, training sessions, one on one, and to large groups of any size, customized training around wellness, personal and professional development.

Mia Turner-Whitley was born to Mr. and Mrs. T Turner! She is married to P. Whitley and they have 7 beautiful children and 12 grandchildren! She has four wonderful siblings, nieces, nephews, great nieces and great nephews and a host of other relatives.

JUST THE FIVE OF US

MIA TURNER-WHITLEY

I pulled up in the driveway of my dark two-story home and just sat in my car in a daze. No one was home at the time. I remember being so numb and in a state of shock. This could not be it, yet it was. I came to the realization that my marriage of 13 years was over. The tears slowly streamed down my face as I sat there contemplating my next move. I had my four babies I had to provide for. How was I going to do that on one salary when together we were in six figures? I remember calling my parents and connecting my siblings to tell them all at once we were getting a divorce. I was met with mixed emotions. A couple said it was about time and the others were empathetic. I remember my parents saying we could move back home to Illinois. I knew one thing; Texas was where I wanted to continue to live and we would be okay. I was going to figure it out with the help of the Lord.

God has a funny way of laughing at our plans. See, I had planned to be married until death parted us, so being a single mom again never crossed my mind. Yet there I was with my teenage daughter, teenage son and two intermediate-aged daughters. I was scared yet determined to make it. I remember one day I was listening to Will Smith's "Just the Two of Us" and I was singing it replacing the "two" with five. It's amazing how songs can give you strength to move forward. Tears well up in my eyes when I hear that song sometimes because it reminds me of the pain and uncertainty I felt for myself and my children during that chapter in my life history. We were all so lost, hurt, and disappointed. My younger ones didn't know what was going on as much as my older ones. They were teens and dealing with their emotions and life changes was enough. Now they had to deal with an event that I know impacted them as much as it did me. The one thing I would recommend to any person going through a divorce, and post-divorce, is to get therapy for you and your children. We didn't do too badly, but it would have helped us to heal properly and navigate our new normal.

Being the "Survivor" (Destiny's Child version), I knew that I had to get myself together real fast for me and my children. I had to somehow mend my broken heart and take care of four children. I didn't know sometimes if I was coming or going. I really think I was a functional mental break-down person. I don't know if you have ever experienced a pain so deep that it ripped you to your core. BUT you have these little people looking up to you to protect them, love them and keep them safe. I could not let them down. In fact, they gave me the strength to go on. I would not ever let them see me stressing over money, or crying, or being upset. I always did that in the privacy of my own bedroom. I would cry and pray and pray and cry. When not around my children I was in a dark and lonely place. Yet to the world I seemed strong and happy. I put on a smile and kept it moving. I am a private person so in order to keep people from being all up in my business, my smile became a mask, except to just a few people I could be the mess I was at that time. It's so important to have trusted confidantes. We will talk more about that later.

So I made a plan. My ex and I decided we would sell our two-story home and move into our own places. In the meantime, he was responsible for the mortgage and I did everything else using unemployment benefits and food stamps. My first step was to find another good paying job where I could afford decent housing and provide for us. I had just completed my undergrad in Psychology and Education. I was hoping to get a job as a pharmaceutical sales representative. This field started out at about 65k and had great perks like bonuses and company car. Interview after interview after interview and no job! Unemployment benefits ran out, so I leaned on other skills. I started substitute teaching while still looking for something that would sustain us while my ex-husband got on my last nerve asking if I had found a place for us to live. This made the whole process so stressful. Often I would wonder how our home that was once a place of love could become so cold.

One day I received a call from a temp agency for Ford Motor Credit for a collection agent. One thing I knew I could do was talk on the phone! I got the job! Good pay! Good benefits! Finally, some good news to help me reach step two of my plan, finding a new home for me and my children. I knew I wasn't financially ready to purchase a home and I had not rented for a minute. I knew I did not want to live in an apartment. I wanted my kids to have their own yard. Nothing against apartment living. We lived in some rather nice apartments a few times. I didn't know where to start!

God blessed me with a wonderful beautician who would treat my hair and scalp. In the midst of going through the divorce my long thick hair began to fall out. It was so scary the rate at which my hair was falling out! My doctor diagnosed me with alopecia which escalated because of the level of stress I was under. A friend of mine said, "Well, at least it's not your mind!" So true, as rough as it was. I did lose a part of me that made it so hard to really go back to trusting a man with all of me. Pieces of me, yes; all of me, NO! I learned that about myself over time. Now that's a whole "nother" book for another time. Well, like most of us we pour our hearts out to our beauticians (the ones you can trust). She was very trustworthy. She knew how sensitive I was about my hair issue so she only would set my appointments for times when other clients were not scheduled. She introduced me to a friend of hers who was a realtor.

I met with him and told him my story through the tears. I didn't have a lot of money and I had to find a safe place for me and my babies. He helped me and I was so grateful. He did a real estate contract for our house. I remember when we sat at our formal dining room table and he went over the contract with me and my ex. There was a point where he advised us of a fee he was waiving because of me and if I changed my mind at any time he would honor, but only if I decided on the change. In that moment, I felt that there are still men with good hearts who want to do nothing, but what's right in helping someone. To this day I am grateful for that moment. It's those little wins that gave me hope. It took us about four months before we found the right home. I completed the application with the application fee and two letters, one from me and one from the realtor. Because I had just started a new job and was recently divorced, we were concerned about my being approved. In the letter my realtor advised me to just speak from my heart and tell them my situation and my desire for home ownership. Although he only knew me for a short time, he wrote a character letter on my behalf. We waited and waited for what seemed forever for a response. They finally they responded, and I was APPROVED!

I felt like our new life was shaping up. I had saved enough for us to get through at least the first couple of months. I didn't tell my ex we were finally vacating until the weekend we were getting ready to move. Another small celebration. I felt that some people thought I was not going to be able to do this on my own. Well, I didn't. God was there with every tear, every let-down, every shut door, and every painful, bitter moment. I prayed! I cried! I was battered, bruised, and broken on the inside. Yet I had to be brave and strong for my children. I would not let them see me looking defeated or sad. I had to be their confident rock. I always felt that children shouldn't have to worry "where will we lay our heads? What will we eat? What will we wear?" So I had to be the strong person I wanted them to be.

My two older children are not by my ex-husband, just my two younger ones. I wanted them all to maintain a level of respect. It was important to me that regardless of what happened between us, I wanted them to have a good relationship. I felt like I was the sole protector of my oldest. It was almost like he either didn't know how to be a part of my older two children's lives, or he divorced them with me. Regarding his son by another mother, he remains as much a part of my family as my own. In fact, I call him son and he calls me mama. When he was told about the divorce he cried like a baby (he was about 12/13 years old). I let him know he would always be a part of my life. We have a very close relationship, and for that I am grateful.

Divorce is not the children's fault. They should not be used as pawns like in a game of chess. They are mini human beings who deserve love, security, and respect. I am not a fan of talking down about the other parent to the child. In most cases it was each of your decision to sleep together and have sex. There is a big chance that a child could come from that moment or moments of pleasure. So their daddy was not that bad a person. Remember that the minute you are about to say, "You act like your old no-good daddy!" You and that old no-good daddy made that life. Instead have people you can confide in and vent to.

Having a strong circle as a parent is so important. Just like it takes a village to raise our children, it takes a trusted circle of real friends to support us. Friends who will let you vent, cry, stare into space and most importantly, will tell you the truth about yourself in love. Shout out to my small circle that I could go to and tell anything, and they listened. They supported me. Thank you so much! Although we don't talk and hang out nearly as much as we did during that time, their strength and support helped me through the most difficult season of my life. They know me and know that no matter what, I will be forever grateful.

It's important to have people who can give you time to breathe by taking the kids for a moment so you can get some self-care. This was one of the hardest things. Getting time for me! Go in the bathroom, what do you hear? "Maaaaaammmmaaaaaa!!!!!!" There was no, "I am going to tell your daddy." You are it! I was it. Some days were harder than others, like the many times when I had more month than money and had to bor-row money just for groceries. Then there is the growing kid syndrome! Every time you turn around, they need a new pair of tennis shoes, or pants. Doing double time going to school when the principal, or teacher called. Making sporting events and practices after working a full shift at work. After playing the sports mom, still having to make sure they eat, do homework, take baths, and have clean clothes for school. The job was never ending. Let's not forget, "Oh Mom, I have a project due tomorrow" and it's 8pm.

I remember one time one of my children was skipping classes so much until we had to go to court. Who didn't have money to pay the city of Arlington, TX was me! As I was sitting in court listening as the other parents went before the judge, I heard this mother say that she did not have the money to pay the ticket. She said it would be unfair for her to have to pay for something that her son did, and the judge agreed! Well, when it was yours truly's turn, I gave the same spiel and the judge agreed. I was grateful for that and of course fussed and talked to my child about the negative consequences of their actions. It was good I didn't have to pay the ticket (I think it was around $500.00). Yet I still had to pay in gas and time, because who was responsible for making sure transportation was available? Right, me! The city we lived in did not have public transportation.

Some days it would be so hectic with three girls and one boy. Yet if it were not for my children, I don't know how I would have made it. They were my life, my reason for continuing to be the best me I could possibly try to be. I will never say I was perfect. I had my flaws and "grown folk desires" for companionship and tried to balance the two. I remember some years after the divorce when my son and I had a heated conversation about bad behaviors. He told me that when I was dating someone it was like they became more important than them. Now that was a gut punch, but his perspective. It really stopped me in my tracks! We had a good heart-to-heart that day that ended in tears, hugs, and apologies on both our parts. I wanted my children to always feel they had a voice and that Mama heard them. I am their biggest supporter, encourager, confidante, and teacher! I tried to make a home where my children didn't have to worry about lack. They had all the basics required by law, a roof over their head, running water, electricity/AC/heat, food, and clothes. I was not the name-brand parent, so as long as following those guidelines were met, we were good.

So here we were, all moved into our own place. That was one of the best feelings! Thanks to my wonderful realtor Mr. Johnson, my kids and I were on our way. Most importantly, we had peace. Peace of mind in our one-story home was everything. Then my brother decided that I didn't need to live in Texas without any family and he moved in with us. For this I was grateful. My brother was and still is a tremendous blessing.

I remember after we moved in and had everything in place, the children were gone to bed, and I became overwhelmed with emotion. It was worse than the ugly cry. I never cried so hard in my life! It was like a release from having to do and accomplish all I did for me and especially my children to get us where we were. We had our own place of refuge. I was able to provide independently for me and my children. FREEDOM! I decided after I let that all out, I would never cry like that again. It was time to put my past in my rear view and move forward. Rear views are especially important. It's just like in our vehicles; we glance at it every now and then to make sure nothing is trying to creep up on us from the back (or the past). We can't move forward only focusing on that rear view. We must keep our main focus on the present and what's ahead.

Now that we were in our own place life was different. I was the boss paying the cost and all the bills. It felt good to make up new rules we didn't have before, like playing any genre of music and not just gospel. Our house became the house where all the kids wanted to be. We were that house! It was so freeing, but then at some time it had to slow down. New rules like curfews had to be implemented. My teenagers were getting a taste of our newfound freedom and curfews as well as discipline had to be put in place.

I will say during that time it was not easy trying to raise a handsome teenage boy with beautiful eyes and a gorgeous smile. He was coming into his manhood and those hormones were on 1000! I remember one time having to go up to the principal's office when he was a freshman in high school. I got there and he met me in the office. I was already upset because I had to take off from work to go up to his school. I asked him what was going on and he was like, "Mama, it's not my fault! I didn't do anything this time." So I am giving him that *yeah, right* look. He proceeds to say, "You remember _____; well, she saw me walking my friend ____ to class and got mad. After school her and a group of her friends went over to the girl's house and told her to come outside so they could fight. Well, her mom was at home and came to the door and addressed the girls with her gun on her person. The girls had words with the mom and finally left." I was just in shock at this girl's boldness and knew obviously something happened between my son and little Miss for her to go beating up people with her squad! Needless to say, the girls were suspended, and my son was sent back to class. After school I had my "sex will always be here" talk with him. I stressed to my teenagers to be single and childless as long as possible.

Well, I became a young grandmother. My daughter, like myself, became a teen parent and a year later so did my son. Now I was not only taking care of my four, but also grandbabies. My daughter took it so hard when I found out she was expecting. She cried so hard and asked me to forgive her. I knew that pain and that cry from when I became a teen parent. All I could do was hold her and tell her we would get through it and everything would be alright.

At that point in my life I was within months of completing my Bachelor's, and then we were in a bad car accident, in which my car was totaled but we all were able to walk away from it. I was so grateful for that. My oldest daughter sustained eye injuries and had to be rushed to the hospital via ambulance. Parkland Hospital in Dallas, TX has some of the best doctors in the country. They took good care of her and were able to save her eye and vision. My younger two took notes from their older siblings and we had no problems.

My children are all adults now. I am proud of all their achievements. My daughter received her cosmetology and culinary arts certification and has an associate degree in business. She teaches her children the importance of entrepreneurship. My son is married, and he is a loving husband and father. My bonus son is doing well also and is in business for himself. My middle daughter has a Bachelor's in Kinesiology and is in ministry school. My baby girl serves in the United States Air Force. I am so proud of the adults they have become and will continue to be.

To a mother who may be going through a rough time being a divorced/single mom, know that tough times really don't last, but tough people do. Love your children by loving yourself first and taking care of you. I knew one day my children would grow up and start adulting, so I prepared myself for the empty nest. I loved on Mia as much as I could when my children were with me. I made time to volunteer at a women's shelter. I eventually found work in the career that I loved. I have been in Customer Service for 26 years to date. Twenty-one of those years have been in Learning and Development in the PBM (Pharmacy Benefit Managers) industry. I am now leading a Leadership Development and Support team in my current organization, where I have been for 14 years. I have earned two master's while being with this organization. My children were still at home when I was earning those degrees while working full time. My wonderful brother was such a Godsend in helping me during that season. He would cook, fuss, support and love us all. I also partnered with a non-profit organization (coming up on 13 years) that believes in the importance of empowering men, women, and children to have healthy relationships. I am the Senior Facilitator in facilitating the following workshops: marriage and engaged couples, parenting, stress and anger management, budgeting (habitudes) and Domestic Violence. Then there's MIA! Motivating, Inspiring/Influencing, Achieving. This is my baby that I thought of during all those trying times, and within the last four years has begun to emerge as MIASpeaks! I am a Transformational Speaker and Author and CEO of my own business. I have also remarried and just celebrated seven years, June 2020, and have two new bonus daughters, a future son-in-law, two bonus grandsons and a host of new relatives!

I said all that to say there is so much greatness in you! If I can do it, so can you! God is not a respecter of persons. So regardless of race, color, or creed, what he does for one, he can do for another. PLEASE find the real you! Be true to her and make time to do the things you love for your own self-worth, self-esteem, and self-care. Losing sight of who you are and what you bring to your own table is the most damaging thing any person can do. Write your own vision of your life. See it. Find scriptures, words and quotes that will strengthen you. Read them over and over and daily. Visualize how you want your life to be and go for it. Know that you will make mistakes, you will fall down, you may even hit rock bottom (if you can look up you can get up), just don't stay there. Acknowledge it and be in that moment. Feel your pain, your hurt, your disappointments, your weaknesses, and flaws (we all have them) and then get up. Reset and reevaluate your goals, set some new ones and keep on pushing forward. I could go on and on! I am so happy for you, sis! I know you are going to bring so much more greatness in the world and will pay my story forward by sharing yours and helping some other mother!

I will end my chapter with one of my favorite verses. Joshua 1:9 (KJV) says, "Be strong and of a good courage; be not afraid, neither be thou dismayed: for the Lord thou God is with thee whithersoever though goest." Amen!

"Motherhood: if you think
my hands are full,
you should see my heart."

– Unknown

Thressa Olivia Dorsey is Founder and Servant Leader of A Listening Heart Ministries, as well as Vibrantly You Coaching as a certified Strategic and Personal Development Life Coach. She is a preacher, teacher, mentor, and woman of prayer who willingly serves in the kingdom as God leads.

Thressa is a published author whose works include Remarkable Faith: Moving Your Faith from Ordinary to Extraordinary, contributing author in The Mom in Me Anthology and will be releasing her next book, Lessons from the Heart in January 2021. She has a passion for seeing people achieve their God-given purpose and living to their highest potential for which they were created. She is grateful and blessed to be a vessel God can use. She is the wife of Tracy Dorsey and mother to Alaina and the late Anton Dorsey. She and her husband are currently living their best lives in Honolulu, Hawai'i.

Auntie Zelda,
Be Blessed ☺
Love,
Thressa Dorsey

DEPRESSION, YOU MESSED WITH THE WRONG DAUGHTER!

THRESSA DORSEY

One of the greatest joys in life is being a mom, should you get the opportunity. Yes, there is good and bad, as well as ups and downs, but nothing is more satisfying to a mom's soul than to see her child/children grow into who they were created to be, to see them become productive, contributing members of society and successful human beings. This is what all moms look forward to, although it is not always a clear path getting there.

My story begins when my daughter went away to college and she encountered mental health struggles. Depression and anxiety had reared their ugly heads again. I found out as a result of receiving the explanation of benefits from our health insurance provider. It was frightening and comforting at the same time. Frightening that she did not share her struggles with her father and me before seeking professional help and comforting that she sought professional help at the moment she needed it.

After receiving the statement, I contacted her to see how things were going and eased my way into asking her about her visits to the mental health clinic on campus. She hesitated for a moment but went on to tell me why she went. I stayed calm and listened attentively. Sometimes this is hard for me to do, but I wanted to be supportive and not reactive.

At times, my reaction to things can be a little intense, but for her sake I knew I shouldn't and couldn't overreact. This was not the time to fall apart and clearly not a time to fuss. My thoughts were all over the place and I had to get my act together so I wouldn't upset my daughter and make her feel like she had done something wrong.

As moms we must recognize our tendency to blow things out of proportion. It does not help, and it could push our child away and cause further damage. Remain calm and let them talk to get things out of their system.

We must take a step back and be grateful for the level of maturity our child showed in reaching out to the right person in their time of need. Just think, things could have taken a turn for the worse.

There are countless stories of parents who were caught off-guard by their child's battle with depression, anxiety, or other mental health issues. The phone call they received was of their child being in the psychiatric ward of a local hospital, strung out on drugs or worse, having met an untimely demise at their own hands. These scenarios will send a shudder through a mother's being just thinking about it.

I was blessed to know my daughter had enough self-awareness and maturity to recognize something was not right. She knew her thoughts were out of sync and took the time to seek help on campus. I applaud her efforts for taking the right path to address her mental health struggles.

It was not an easy road to travel for her. Although we had been down this road before, this time things were different. My daughter attended the University of Maryland College Park and lived on campus. She was a little over 33 miles from home and I had to accept this for the next four years. Her father and I made sure we traveled to visit her and do different activities with her as a family. Later it hit me that it would take at least 40-45 minutes to get to her in the event of an emergency. It didn't give me a warm and fuzzy feeling once I realized the magnitude of what was going on. *Okay Thressa, don't panic; things will work out just fine.*

Think about that for a moment. Your child calls and tells you they need help because they are in a crisis and it takes you nearly an hour to get to them. This is not taking into account that you must get dressed, get in the car, navigate traffic (on 95 and 495), get on the campus, find somewhere to park and then get to their dorm room. It is enough to cause you to have an anxiety attack and heart attack at the same time.

Yet as moms, we will do whatever it takes to ensure our children are safe, healthy, and whole. I had to do some soul searching and personal evaluation in order to develop a plan of action for my daughter and walk with her through this.

Later, it came to me that there was a bright side. The realization dawned on me that I was closer to my daughter from where I worked. With decent traffic it took around 20-25 minutes to get to the campus. With this discovery I could arrange to meet up with her when she finished her classes for the day. We could get together after I got off work, because it made more sense to drive to the campus from work than to go home and come back over the weekend, especially if we wanted to do a mother/daughter hangout.

When faced with my child dealing with mental illness, I really did not know what to do. Although this encounter was a couple years after the first, I was beside myself. There were moments when I felt like I was having an out-of-body experience. There were times when I would question my sanity. I began to think, *Whose side of the family did this come from? Why is this happening to my child? Why is this happening to me? Okay Lord what are you trying to teach me? Because right now I'm not getting it.* I prayed and cried, cried, and prayed. The Lord gave me peace and lifted me when I felt at my lowest.

I did my best to try and make some sense out of what was going on. Yes, we had been down the road of depression before, but this experience was new territory for me. My daughter was 33 miles from home, living in a dorm room the size of a postage stamp, she did not have a car, and was subject to the whim of the monster attacking her mind at any given moment.

The first experience with her depression in high school was different. She was at home and her bedroom was across the hall. If she was struggling, I was right there, just a few feet away and not 33 miles. We may have chit-chatted and even jokingly talked about depression in my family, but not any in-depth conversation. It was not really talked about in African American families. Well, at least not mine.

How many can say that they had real, heart-to-heart discussions with their family and friends about mental health? Go ahead while you are thinking... I'll wait. Not until recently did African Americans, especially women, sit down to talk about the state of our minds. We witnessed firsthand and saw our grandmothers, mothers, aunts, sisters, cousins, and neighbors living the Black Superwoman Syndrome. In our eyes there was nothing they could not handle!

To us they did it all, carried it all, made it all, had it all and admitting they needed help was considered a sign of weakness. In turn, they passed that behavior on to us and we perpetuated the cycle and would eventually pass it on to our daughters. It was time for the myths and the lies to stop! These beliefs were causing our black women to have nervous breakdowns, heart attacks, strokes, and even commit suicide.

As my daughter struggled with her mental wellbeing, it hit me that I had my own mental health struggles to deal with as well. However, I ended up putting my thought life on the back burner in order to make sure my daughter's thought life was healed.

I was elated that my daughter would be the first on my side of the family to attend college. We talked about college to both of our children from the time they were small children. It was a regular conversation and an affirmation we instilled in them that this would be a normal way of life. College would not be an afterthought but a planned event.

Both of my children, son, and daughter were creative and exceptionally talented. My son could make clothing from scraps and without a pattern. He also danced, designed clothing, put on fashion shows, and would later enter the music business as a rapper. My daughter learned to read at the age of three, loved books, wrote poetry and short stories, and studied Japanese in middle school, high school, and college. She was an amazing artist. Matter of fact, she still is.

In my research I discovered when some persons are highly creative and talented it can and does influence their mental health. The mind of a creative is pretty much in motion all the time. Sleep can be disrupted, and it is as if the mind never slows down or shuts off. The reason I know this is I am a creative and my children got many of their traits from me. Depression decided to mess with my daughter in her late teens.

The initial experience came when my daughter, the younger of the two, was in senior high school. One day while at work, I received a phone call from her high school nurse. She did her introduction, told me why she was calling and proceeded to put my daughter on the phone. My daughter told me she felt unstable and her voice was shaking. I wasn't quite sure what she meant so I asked her to give me a few more details. I told her I would be there to pick her up once I spoke with my supervisor and we would go to seek professional help.

Once I got off the phone, I went to my supervisor and told him I had a family emergency and would be leaving for the day. After getting to my car, I looked up the phone number for the counseling center run by the church I was attending at the time. To the glory of God, I was able to get a same-day appointment. The other blessing is that it was less than five minutes from my daughter's school and once I picked her up our next stop was there.

We were received as soon as we walked in, I completed insurance paper-work, and she was seen by a counselor for an initial assessment. About 30-40 minutes later my daughter and the counselor returned and a course of treatment was discussed. We stopped at the front desk, scheduled the next appointment, and went home.

While at home, we had a brief conversation centered around what hap-pened and the next steps. My daughter shared her feelings and what prompted the trip to the nurse's office and the phone call to me at work. I listened and assured her we would do whatever was necessary to get her through this rough patch she was dealing with. She went to her room to lie down.

As my daughter rested, I was trying to convince myself everything was going to be okay. Later that evening, as I tried to calm my own anxious mind, a million thoughts ran through my head. Amid what was going on with my daughter, I had to do some soul searching.

Depression does not just affect the person it attacks, it also has an effect on those around them, especially their family and most definitely Mom. My mind was inundated with the ugliest thoughts. I shuddered at think-ing she might attempt suicide or have to take anti-psychotic medication or an anti-depressant or have to be committed to a mental hospital. My mind was all over the place and this was just the first episode I dealt with. What's a mother to do?

I had to get it together. I was already putting my child on drugs, in a mental institution and worse, committing suicide, and this was just our first encounter. *Okay, focus Thressa, focus. Take things one step, one day at a time; the day isn't over yet.* I could hear my grandmother's voice saying, "Slow down and trust God; everything will work out fine."

Leaning on my faith was one of the things that kept me going. The most important part of my belief system was prayer. Growing up I watched my grandmother go before the Kingdom of Heaven and petition on our family's behalf. What was most astounding was getting to witness the answers to the prayers she prayed. This is what I held on to as we walked through this valley together. Prayer is the key and faith unlocks the door.

On this journey, I had to do some homework to understand what I was dealing with. Following are some of the symptoms for depression in teens. Those in bold were those my daughter suffered with. *Sadness,* ***irritability,*** *feeling negative and worthless, anger, poor performance or poor attendance at school,* ***feeling misunderstood and extremely sensitive,*** *using recreational drugs or alcohol, eating or sleeping too much,* ***self-harm,*** ***loss of interest in normal activities, and*** ***avoidance of social interaction.***

What was amazing was her grades remained A's and B's, she played community sports (soccer and softball), yet somehow, she was fighting a monster attempting to overwhelm her mind. Yet, her resilience let me know God was still at work in her life.

Even when she was in college, she managed to keep up her grades. I believe she may have failed one class and would later make it up to pass. She didn't take any time off except during the Summer and for scheduled breaks. Her father and I made certain to provide whatever support she needed to get her across that stage in four years.

I adjusted some areas of my life to be available when needed. It was not easy, but it all worked out. Depression messed with the wrong daughter, and this mom was ready to take him on.

Being a mom means we will do most anything for our children and having to help your child through a tough situation will cause sleepless nights and days of aimlessly peering off into the distance. It can be overwhelming and draining. Yet it is during these periods when we discover there is a well deep within where we can find strength. It is at our lowest moments when this reservoir reveals the unlimited source of its contents. It is in these times when God's strength is made perfect in our weakness.

The lives of our children are in our hands. We have been given the role and responsibility of teaching, guiding, correcting, encouraging, and nurturing them into adulthood. We can read countless books, watch this movie and that documentary, but none of those things will make a difference if we don't watch and listen.

It is not necessary to know what our children are doing each waking moment, but we should know something about who they are at the core. We must study our children, get to know what makes them tick, and what they need from us as their mom.

I thought I knew how to parent both of my children and tried to do it the way I was parented. Sorry, many things did not work, and it made me have to go back to the drawing board to learn what would stay and what had to go. We cannot raise our sons like we do our daughters and we cannot raise our daughters like we do our sons. They are different. They are individuals with their own personalities, traits, and quirks. We have to meet them where they are, not where we want them to be.

There are basic values we should instill in them: Love God, love people, and love themselves. Also, be kind, go to college, get a well-paying job, save money, help others, and pay your bills on time. We are to assist them in getting ready for adulthood. This includes a discussion on taking care of their mental health.

If I knew then what I know now, I would have gotten a regimen going to regularly check in with my daughter and ask how she was doing mentally. It didn't have to be every day, but nonetheless it would be part of our mother/daughter chats. The goal should have been to be proactive and not just reactive when a crisis arose.

As we moved through that first encounter and the visits to the counselor became fewer and she appeared to be back to "normal," I slacked off and let things go by the wayside. I stopped checking on her and asking about her mental wellbeing and went on with life.

It's not that I didn't care; it was more "out of sight, out of mind (no pun intended)." She seemed to be doing okay. She participated in senior events, went to her prom, walked across the stage and got her diploma, so now it was time to prepare for college. She was excited, we were excited, and the depression was nowhere to be found, or so I thought.

Although I researched and read about teenage depression before, truly little of the information was retained. I remembered a few of the symptoms but not all of them. For the most part I didn't give it much attention because I thought it was all behind us. What it was doing was waiting for the opportune moment to strike again and attempt to take my daughter out. Part of my personal routine was to pray for my children daily and I did that. My children were bathed in prayer throughout the day, but that didn't mean the attacks would just suddenly stop or go away without notice.

Mom, you can do this and make it to the other side with flying colors! Your child will get through this and will come out stronger than they were before. This is not the time to give up, give out or give in. You can, and you will be okay.

Don't be as hard on yourself as I was. I carried the burden of guilt and shame, because I thought I didn't do a good job of raising my daughter and her battling depression was the result. When your flesh and blood is faced with struggles in mental health, the weight of the circumstance can nearly render you powerless. Don't fall for it; give it your all and don't forget to call on your tribe to support you.

When your child is facing off with an unseen and unpredictable enemy it can make you want to put up your hands and throw in the towel. But not today. Nope, sorry, can't do that! Just like at the bottom of Pandora's Box, there is still hope for recovery. Your child will overcome and continue on to live their best life. It will not happen overnight, in a few days, in several weeks or in a few months or even in a year, but it will happen. Victory is on the horizon.

Even in the darkest moments, look for a glimmer of light. When your child is struggling and can't seem to cope, pray for peace in their mind and in their heart. As you are taking care of everyone else, don't forget to take care of yourself.

I'm proud to say that my daughter finished college on time in four years and graduated May 2011 with a Bachelor's in Japanese and a Certificate in East Asian Studies. As she walked across the stage my heart was full of gratitude because she and I knew what it took for her to get there. It was a great day and depression realized it had messed with the wrong daughter!

"There are places
in the heart
you don't even know exist
until you love a child."

– **Anne Lamott**

Margo W. Williams is a Relationship & Conflict Coach, Minister, Ministry Consultant, Author, and Public Speaker. She earned a B.S. in Marketing and a B.S. in Insurance & Economic Security from the University of South Carolina. Later, she received a Master of Divinity from Columbia International University Seminary and School of Missions. Currently, Mrs. Williams is a Doctoral Candidate at Erskine Theological Seminary with an emphasis on Conflict Resolution and Restoration. She is dedicated to edifying and strengthening the lives of those who struggle with walking in the power of God due to unresolved hurt and disappointments. This passion led her to write *Petty Pain: Understanding the Assignment of Offense.*

For more than 23 years, Mrs. Williams has provided Biblical Counseling to men and women, with special emphasis on resolving various types of conflict, inner healing, and communication. Along with her husband, she established a Couples Ministry. Margo is the Founder of Graceful Fire and Margo W. Williams Ministries, a registered 501(c)3. Together, she serves the Kingdom in the areas of teaching, preaching, ministry consultation, leadership and discipleship coaching and training, and global missions. She is a licensed and ordained Baptist Minister.

"MIRROR, MIRROR ON THE WALL..."

MARGO W. WILLIAMS

I remember being a little girl who watched the "Wonderful World of Disney" on Sunday evenings. I loved to see reruns of all the Disney princesses, but my favorite was Snow White and the Seven Dwarfs. Instead of admiring Snow White, I found the evil queen to be fascinating. I was always amazed at her sense of insecurity. Snow White was her stepdaughter and she was jealous of her beauty. Daily she would awaken with the fear of being intimidated, and anger towards the one she should have loved. Instead of setting the confident example of royalty, she questioned her value and purpose. The evil queen would look into her mirror and ask, "Mirror Mirror, who is the fairest in the land?" Rather than embracing who she was and accepting her kingdom position, she focused on Snow White. The queen was unsure of who she really was.

I grew up having a strong understanding of who I was, and the power I had to become whatever I chose to be. There were times I allowed the criticisms of others to affect my view of myself, so I relied on the portrait painted by those who loved me the most: parents, grandparents, aunts, and uncles. Family was a priority to me and as far back as I can remember, I always knew I was called to serve others and be a wife and mother. I saw myself as a lawyer or teacher, and missionary. This was an unrelenting belief which was seeded within my being from the time I was a little girl.

I recall studying my mother, grandmothers, and aunts. It was interesting and fascinating to learn how they were equipped to handle the pressures of being wives and mothers. It seemed so simple. I would sit on the toilet seat and watch my mom put on her makeup. By the time I was in elementary school, I would pucker my lips for a touch of gloss. I took copious heart notes of our family holiday meals; they were delicious to eat and perfectly pleasing to the eyes. As soon as I was given the green light, I stood up in a kitchen chair and began to mix the favored macaroni and cheese casserole. All I knew was that I was on my way to be like them: the women I adored. My aunts were educators, entrepreneurs, soldiers, factory workers and housewives. Each, in her own way, deposited a piece of herself into my life. I certainly have been blessed.

My mother was complex in nature; therefore, I am inadequate in classifying her status. She was known to be the neighborhood "good gangster" who would dare to say and do what others would merely think about. I remember putting my fingers in my ears or sinking in the seat when she would give someone a "piece of her mind." My mother didn't have a problem standing 4'11" in her size seven shoes. She didn't bother anyone, but when she saw injustice, she would handle business like a champ. This same woman lovingly attended to our needs and kept us in check. In the strangest sort of way, it was my mother's intricate nature that taught me to love the Lord, stand up for myself, do my best, respect myself, honor authority, and walk in grace. She could sing first soprano like a bird and was a part of the church choir. She loved the arts and made great attempts at developing me into a musician, but I never grew to embrace practicing the piano.

As a daughter, it was important for me to please my parents, so I tried to avoid disappointing them. For this reason, I blindly walked a few bumpy paths which led to nowhere. At the forefront of my life was an obligation to make them happy and proud. Like most young people, I wanted to explore and enjoy the things teenagers craved. The problem was that anytime I would sneak and try things, most of the time I got caught. I recall being on punishment for going somewhere I was told not to go. My parents took my car keys and grounded me for two weeks.

When my maternal grandfather approached me about my punishment, he chuckled and said, "God's trying to help you." Granddaddy began to tell me stories about my mother's younger years and how she was smart, strong-willed, and often rebellious. He said, "Watch your step." I wasn't entirely sure what that meant but I was clear that parental acceptance and approval was still my choice.

I came to understand that it was a fallacy to believe I had the power to determine my parents' decisions. During our engagement, this delusion was threatened when my mother rejected the idea that we were getting married out of town and not in the church and community I was raised in. She told me that she was not coming to our wedding. Of course, I wasn't ready to hear that, but it became a valuable **life lesson**. After wiping the tears, I stood up to my mother and moved forward with our wedding plans. For weeks I spoke to the little girl and teenager inside me, the one who craved the smiles, the nods, and the applause from her parents. Eventually, however, the adult within assured me that life would go on with or without her blessing. I had no control over my mother's decision, but I had total control of how I chose to respond to her choice. Needless to say, three months before the big day, my mother got on board and began to help with the wedding plans.

The next **life lesson** was learned as a wife. Soon after the honeymoon phase, I glanced into the internal mirror of my being and didn't recognize myself. I was a wife, but who was she? I didn't like what I saw because the image wasn't the reflection I was looking for. I realized I had spent most of my life living within the lines which had been established for me. I had literally become what "they wanted" and not who I really was. Unfortunately, I didn't know the person I had become. I began to measure my life by silent disappointments, hurts and pains. Before long, I was angry with myself. That anger evolved into depression and I felt obliged to keep it to myself. It was not something the women in my family ever spoke about. Looking back, their silence was symbolic of their denial, protection, and survival. Like me, I believe they lost themselves in the process of being who and what was expected of them.

My message as a mother began to unfold as I entered marriage. Note the expression: as I entered married life. I found that marriage is the process of learning how to be compatible in a committed relationship. As we entered the marriage journey, my husband and I had philosophies of what a marriage would look like, and they weren't based upon the concrete knowledge of God's Word. We brought the sum totals of our lives together, shook them up at the altar, and created an image of what we wanted and not what God had ordained. Both of us, in our individual selves, were the products of our upbringings. My husband admittedly declared that he didn't have any image of a good marriage in his family. At that time few married and if they did, they ended in divorce. My life was the opposite. All around me were married couples and I only knew of four divorces.

Again, bringing my past into the present, I worked hard to present myself as the wife who would make my husband proud. I learned quickly that fairytales were written for books and that real life was a tale of tests, trials, and triumphs. On the day I looked into that mirror, I saw a distorted image. I had become a stranger to myself. I wasn't happy and didn't know the correct path to get there. I had grossly neglected myself. What were my dreams, goals, and aspirations? I couldn't remember what I liked because I was busy working, cooking, tending house and being the good wife and mother. The question remained: "Who am I?" The thought of discussing how I felt was literally insulting because I was supposed to have it together. I didn't. In my mirror were two people competing in one body. One woman was becoming her mother, grandmothers, and aunts, and the other was searching for herself.

Motherhood has been a stark reminder of the power and value of knowing self. In William Shakespeare's Hamlet, Polonius advises his son, "To thine own self be true." As long as I was living my life to please everyone around me, I was incapable of becoming my authentic self. When we are authentic, we are who and what we claim ourselves to be. The problem arises when we are unable to adequately identify who or what we are. Having children challenged my inner vows, and having a daughter forced me to discover the origin of my truths. The path of parenting is paved with stones and fragments of all the words and experiences of life, whether they are great or small, good, or bad.

I imagined and prayed to one day have a daughter, and Morgan became the answer to my prayers. In my mind I thought she would look like my sister and share my interests and opinions. By the time she was four years old I had a glimpse of her independence and resilient nature. I recall receiving a call from her preschool, asking me to come in for a conference. I stopped what I was doing and went to the school. Morgan was sitting in a chair in the headmaster's office patiently waiting for me. I was told that she and Kennedi had misbehaved during naptime. When each was questioned about what had transpired Kennedi was compliant, but Morgan wasn't. The headmaster described Kennedi as being very remorseful; she apologized and cried. Morgan's response was the opposite. She said that Morgan answered her questions and refused to apologize or talk about the incident any further, so she was sending her home to "think about it" for a few days. When we got home, I asked Morgan to explain what happened during naptime. She confidently stated, "You heard Ms. Ina. We didn't do anything wrong. They are making a big something and it was nothing. I'm not talking about it anymore. I told Ms. Ina that. Momma, I'm not talking about it." She wouldn't talk any further about their harmless shenanigans and she chose to go to her room and nap. Although she loved school, she was content to miss two days because of this issue. I recall the mixed emotions of pride and concern. I was proud to know that Morgan was an independent thinker who could stand up for herself and not easily be swayed. I was concerned that her self-assured nature could become a tool the enemy would use against her if she didn't have humility and spiritual discernment.

As Morgan entered puberty, she became secretive and silent. By this time, she knew what behavior was acceptable and what wasn't. She also had become aware of life outside of our family bubble. I was unaware she had been deeply hurt by two women at church, who repeatedly commented on her size. Like her mother, at that age, her body looked three years older than her age. This was an issue of genetics. She began to question her worth, feeling that something was wrong with her because she was larger than her peers. She would act out by putting makeup on at school and using her allowance to buy grownup clothes. By the time she went to high school her mind was clogged with boys, dance, basketball, and how to get away with the next trick. Some weeks my husband and I had to become FBI agents to determine what she was up to before we gave her permission to go anywhere without us. She was quite busy doing some of the things I would have done at that age if I had not been so committed to making my parents so happy. I saw myself in the mirror.

My reckoning came the day my husband called and told me our home had been robbed. When reporting this to the police it became clear that our daughter had a strong suspicion of who had violated our personal sanctuary. As I listed the items that were taken, I began to weep at the thought of my engagement ring being pawned for quick cash. At the time, she was sorry for her disobedience; she apologized but continued to sneak around. This was the first of several situations that worked to threaten Morgan and our family. I would often question God about her wayward behaviors. In my frustration, I said to my husband, "I don't know where she got this from. I was an obedient child. I would have never done the things Morgan keeps doing." He winced and said, "She is not you." This opened an intense dialog which changed my life as a mother and wife. Later that night and for days, I asked God to show me myself. He began to bring memories of things I wanted to do but chose not to because of my family. He also reminded me of the times I crossed the lines and didn't get caught. Suddenly, I began to sober up in my assessment of this child "who was not like her mother." I had spent so much of my life trying to live up to the expectations of others that I got lost in the shuffle of their lives. Now the crucial time had come for me to confront me. "Mirror, mirror on the wall, what is it that I see?" I saw a woman who had become a strong and resilient soul, who put her family first in all she did. She had learned to function under the guise of imagery. This woman was secure in her abilities to help others while courteously walking in distress. I hadn't given myself permission to fail or feel. I had learned to be like my mother, grandmothers, and aunts. The mirror said that I handled being a wife and mother with ease because that was expected of me.

I saw a woman who had bought the lies that I had to be a good girl, color inside the lines, and make my family proud. All these realizations are valuable, but they must be relevant. I began to perform an archaeological dig of my values and it became a dirty exercise in truth. What did it mean to be a "good girl?" What is an accurate measure of good? Who told me I had to "color inside the lines?" Did that mean it was unnatural for me to break the rules or go against the norm? Did I believe I would be loved less because I disappointed or embarrassed my parents? Did I equate my self-worth with their approval? These questions began to rattle the foundation of my being. I learned that I expected my daughter to be like me because that was all I knew. It also meant that somehow, I was afraid that she would become the daughter who chose to deviate from the obligation of how mothers, grandmothers, and aunts were to behave. I realized I had never opened my heart to find out what made me believe my way of being was the only way to be. My husband was incorrect when he reminded me that our daughter was not like me. It became clear that I had chosen to suppress my true thoughts and emotions and Morgan was more honest in her expressions. Although some of her behaviors were a little extreme, the lesson had more to do with inward truths. Morgan never denied who she was for the sake of another. While this fact may appear selfish, it is liberating.

For several years I was so lost in Morgan's quest to break the rules that I believe it caused her to feel more empowered. The Holy Spirit dug up a few artifacts of mine where I colored outside the lines. In my imperfections I saw a thread of similarities between my daughter and myself. It became humorous to see how blinded I had been by my self-inflicted pressure to be perfect. By the time our daughter became a young adult she had matured enough to make better choices, but she is certain of the importance of being herself. She taught me the valuable lesson of living in freedom, of knowing and honoring myself. Today, when I look in the mirror, I see a woman who embraces truth and refuses fallacy. She no longer stays inside the lines, nor does she care to follow the norm. She is strong and weak; flawed and perfect; and one who is released to be her true self. My daughter was and remains a reflection of myself.

Looking in the mirror, two dominant factors held me hostage: a false understanding of the love of God and self-righteousness. Deep inside my soul, I had a false understanding of a loving God. As a child, I was always afraid that God would violently discipline me for thinking or doing bad things. I focused on being nice, pleasant, respectful, and gracious. There shouldn't be anything wrong with these qualities, or so I thought. To be clear, these virtues are the dominant part of my God-given personality. The problem came in when I didn't leave any room for anything else. Looking into the mirror of Morgan's soul, I learned that it's all right to not be all right. In a strange sort of way, I believe the Lord was delivering me from myself with each rebellious antic Morgan used as she was growing up. It was never His will for me to house my soul in the walls of suppression. All those things I chose not to do were really placed before me to teach me the value in knowing who I was, and to confidently stand 5'4" in my nine shoes. I learned from my daughter that positive and negative emotions are both necessary to our self-awareness. They are merely tools to gauge where we are emotionally, psychologically, physically, relationally, and spiritually. Morgan gave herself permission to emote and feel, and I unknowingly was trying to suppress those feelings.

"Making the decision to have a child – it is momentous. It is to decide forever to have your heart go walking around outside your body. "

– Elizabeth Stone

Trailblazer, Compassionate and Dedicated are just a few words to describe the life and journey of Tamira N. Dunn. The founder of Dream Girls Mentoring Program, Incorporated, Tamira is a 32-year-old native Baltimorean raised with her younger brother by a single mom. She attended Baltimore County Schools and graduated from Parkville High School in 2004. After high school, she attended Morgan State University where she received her Bachelors of Science degree in Psychology in 2008. She decided to further her education and received a Master of Science degree in Human Service Administration from University of Baltimore.

Ms. Dunn's passion for the youth and community started while she was in high school. She was always trying to find a way to "make a difference". Watching many of her peers and close friends have children at a young age; she felt it necessary to provide a program that would deliver resources and support to young moms. Ms. Dunn has received many citations from Mayor Stephanie Rawlings Blake and Senator Barbara Mikulski. She has also been awarded a resolution from Council President Bernard Jack Young's office for her countless efforts towards bettering the lives of teen moms. She is a part of the Women of Power Organization and received her award in 2011 and was awarded Top 30 under 30 by 92Q Jams. She also served on the Baltimore City Youth Commission as the Health Committee Chair and a member of the Recs and Parks Committee.

Devastated by the loss of her son, Ms. Dunn Co- Founded Elijah's Hope Foundation Inc. The foundation sponsors an annual walk for pregnancy and infant loss in Baltimore and donates a portion of the proceeds to their scholarship fund which supports doctoral students who are majoring in women and reproductive health. The loss of her son was very heartbreaking, but she has used her passion for helping others to create a resource for women who have experienced the same loss. "Life after loss was very, very hard for me and therapy was a way to find my true self," she says. A year after her loss, she accepted a position at Roberta's House as the Program Manager for the Hope Project. The Hope Project provides supportive services to women who have experienced a fetal or infant loss before the child's first birthday. Ms. Dunn is truly using her testimony to help others. Her goal is to empower women to keep the faith despite their loss. In 2018, she was awarded a social innovation fellowship from the Warnock Fellowship for her idea of building an app to support women through the grieving process who have had a pregnancy or infant loss.

Two years after Ms. Dunn's miscarriage, she became a foster parent to her now 3-year old daughter and she gave birth to her rainbow baby. Ms. Dunn is currently working to rebirth the Baltimore City Resource Parent Association through the Department of Social Services. Tamira wants to ensure that all foster parents have their voices heard and have a seat at the table.

Ms. Dunn is a member of Zeta Phi Beta Sorority Inc. She has dedicated countless hours as a community servant with the Mayor's Office during many youth events. Motivated by the quote, "Be the change that you wish to see in the world" by Mahatma Gandhi, Ms. Dunn wishes to continue to encourage, uplift, and motivate children, youth and families.

MY JOURNEY AS A SINGLE MOM

TAMIRA DUNN

I never would have thought in a million years I would ultimately consider a path that is often shunned, especially in the African American community. You hear so many stories about black children being raised by single mothers and how different the quality of life is for those children, how being raised by a two-parent home is the best option for children and anything different than that suggests that children will most likely fail as a result of being raised by a single mom.

However, that was not my story. At 33 years old, I am proud to say I am a product of a single parent. Having graduated from college with not only my Bachelor's degree but a Master's degree as well, I have excelled in every aspect of my professional career. I'd known I wanted to be a mom for years. I helped my friends with their children when I had none of my own. I liked to think of myself as the fairy godmother.

I struggled with finding love or what love was supposed to look like. Growing up with a single mother, there was no real example of how a man should love a woman. I knew that I wanted to be a mom and I knew that I wanted to be married. I didn't have a preference as to order. Marriage before children was not something I lived my life by. I wanted to be happy, and if being a mom first was the path I was led to, then I would embrace it.

Some would say I was an overachiever and had a lot going for myself. Deep down, I wasn't fulfilled. I worked hard because I wanted to be successful and I believed I was doing just that. College grad, business owner, own car, home, great friends—the list goes on. I often would ask myself, what next!? Where do I go from here? Professionally I was thriving but personally, my life was at a standstill.

It was spring 2014, I was getting ready to graduate with my Master's degree and I opened my first summer camp, where I had enrolled over 50 children! I was uber-excited to not only graduate with another degree but to have the opportunity to work for myself.

Entrepreneurship is something I strived toward for many years. In 2008 I started my first nonprofit that worked directly with pregnant and parenting teens. I had longed for the opportunity where I could wake up every day and go to work for myself. The summer of 2014, I was able to do just that.

So here I was fresh out of grad school, working for myself, single with no children! Seemed like the perfect summer! I realized that since school had ended, I wanted to start dating. I eventually wanted to get married and start a family. *Where do I start? Do I go out more? Do I try online dating? What?* I decided to try online dating. There were so many apps to try but the one that was popular was POF (Plenty of Fish). I can't remember how long I was on there, but I eventually met a guy and we connected instantly. He was handsome, intelligent and someone I thought I would be with long term.

We started dating and hanging out all the time. He didn't work far from the camp so there were times he would come to the camp on his lunch break. We had become really good friends. What started off great ended in trauma. As our relationship progressed, I found out in August that I was pregnant. I had mixed feelings because we had just met in March. I felt irresponsible because we weren't "official," and there was still so much I had to learn about him. I knew that no matter what, I would be a great mom. This was my first pregnancy, so I didn't know what to expect. I went to all my scheduled doctor's appointments, took my vitamins, and stayed active as much as possible. My child's father at the time started to embrace the pregnancy and was very supportive.

The morning I turned 15 weeks is the same morning my pregnancy ended. I was devastated, depressed, and heartbroken. I felt like my world had ended. I was on such a hot streak in the beginning of 2014, but it ended with so much trauma and heartache.

I went through the grieving process and while I was grieving the loss of my son, I was also grieving the loss of what could have been with my son's dad. Our relationship was so new, and we were still learning each other, so when we lost the baby, we had a hard time getting back to us. I struggled with the relationship because there were so many signs that indicated that I should leave, but because of what we had in the beginning, I wanted to hold on.

It wasn't until we had a conversation about having more children that I knew I needed to end the relationship and move forward. I knew I wanted to be a mom. I had always cared for other children and I would probably call myself "godmother of the year." I was accomplished yet felt so empty. I had so much going on for myself, but I longed to be a mother, even more so after the loss. There were times I thought I couldn't have children, so to be able to conceive and have the pregnancy end was heartbreaking. I struggled with my 'so now what' for months. And after my "relationship" ended, I started on my journey to become a single mother....by choice.

I know you're probably thinking I'm crazy, right? Who wants to parent alone? I never thought I would be that person, but it turns out this was the path I was supposed to take. I first started with becoming a foster mom in 2016. I started the classes in late 2015 and was finally finished in February 2016. My first placement was a six-week old baby boy with big brown eyes. He was so handsome! I knew that the placement would only be temporary because he was scheduled to go to court the following week; however, I was in awe. I finally held a baby. It felt so weird yet so comforting. That entire week I had the opportunity to care for a child and it felt so good.

Just like I knew, he would be going to live with relatives the following week. It stung a little but after a day or so, I was okay. I didn't know how long it would be until my next placement, so I started thinking of other options. I had a conversation with my mother, who suggested I look into in vitro fertilization. My first reaction was, "What, you want me to get pregnant by a sperm donor?" She told me that it was more common than I thought and that if having a baby was something I wanted, I should do my research, so I did. I researched, read blogs, articles and more about what was called single mother by choice. I thought to myself, *no way this will work,* but it didn't stop me from trying. I set my plan in motion and before I knew it, the process of becoming a mom was starting.

Right in the middle of the process I got a call from the department of social services; another child was on their way to my home. I was excited because this one was an infant too. She was five months old and would be with me for longer than a week.

As time went on, I continued with my process of becoming a mom. I didn't know how long the child I had would be with me, so I didn't think there was any need to put my plan on hold.

I had the support of my family and close friends so I wasn't worried about whether or not I could do it. I prayed and asked God that if it was meant to be, the procedure would work on the first try, and it did. I got an IUI done in April and was pregnant in May of 2016. I cried because it actually worked.

Today I am a proud single mom of two beautiful girls, one I birthed and one that God saw fit for me to raise. Five years ago, I had no idea I would be on a single motherhood journey. I wanted to be married and have children but after my miscarriage, my plan for a traditional family changed. Life was too short, and I was not going to live my life based on other people's opinions or feelings. There were people who told me it wasn't in God's plan for me to be a single mother and that I needed to just wait because my time would come. But how did they know what God's plan was for me? I am a woman of faith and I know that God has a different plan for us all. This plan I'm on may not be ideal and may make others uncomfortable, but I have always gone after what I wanted, and this situation was no different.

I loved my children so much that I wanted them more than I wanted any relationship. There are days I ask myself if I did the right thing, and the answer is yes. I have no idea where I would be if it were not for my two daughters. This journey is not easy, and of course there are times I wish I had help, but just like God blessed me with these girls, I know he's going to bless me with a partner that will be here to help around the clock. I did things out of order and that's okay. I went with what my heart wanted. Could I have waited? Of course, I could have, but why did I have to? I think about if I had waited, I would have never met my daughter that I didn't birth.

Why are we afraid to go after what we want? Are we too consumed with what others will say? How do we move past the judgment? Throughout my life I've learned that those who judge the steps and path you take are the ones who are scared they didn't think of it first. I did not wake up one day and say, "I want to be a single mom," but tragedy hit home, and not knowing if I would ever have that chance made me focus on what I really wanted.

I'm encouraging all single moms, whether by choice or force, to not think of your situation as a handicap. Use it as your platform for greater. Crush those goals like no one is watching and take your children on the ride with you. You don't stop working because you're a single mom; you just go harder because you have people looking up to you.

 LaRay M. Williams is a four-time graduate of the University of Maryland Global Campus, she earned two Bachelor of Science degrees in Human Resources and Management Studies, an Associate of Arts degree in Human Resources, and a professional certificate in Human Resources. She attributes success to her trust in God, her parents unwavering support, and the village God placed in her life.

Sometimes, life choices can steer you off course, and challenge you to set a course for success "in spite of " your circumstances. LaRay found herself in uncharted territory at the age of sixteen when she became a single parent. She is the mother of two children, and Nannan to her grandchildren and great niece.

An avid reader, traveler, and baker, LaRay is also a dedicated volunteer to both her local church (leading the Women's ministry and teaching Bible Study) and Partners in Care. She enjoys mentoring young women and spending time with family.

EVERYONE NEEDS A CHAMPION

LARAY WILLIAMS

"I had a dream about fish; that girl is pregnant." That is how the conversation started on Mother's Day 1983. My mother defended me to my grandmothers until she could not anymore.

I clearly remember the night my mother told me we were going to the OB/GYN to see how far along I was in my pregnancy. She came into my room, sat beside me, and said, "Tomorrow after your driving test, we are going to the doctor." I asked her why, and she said, "You know why. I need to know how far along you are in your pregnancy so we can prepare. Your volleyball coach called me, and she thinks you are pregnant; that is why she will not let you play this year."

Well, the next day was full of mixed emotions – I received my driver's license and waiting for me were my mother and boyfriend. All smiles, I said, "I did it!" My mom's response was, "Great, now, you can drive us to the doctor." I was not happy; he just looked at me with a silly grin on his face. I denied being pregnant right until the doctor took one look at me and said, "She is carrying the baby in her back." After the examination, she told me I was about five months along. She explained to us that I was carrying the baby in my back and because I was so young, my body adjusted; it was only when I lay on my back and side that my pregnancy showed. Right after I found out, my body betrayed me and exploded, I really was five months pregnant. Sixteen and pregnant—it was not a TV show; it was my reality.

The responses to my pregnancy were mixed, from being supportive to discouraging. As my parents sat down with me and the father of my unborn child, they explained their disappointment and support at the same time. The next day, we had a family meeting with his parents. They were shocked but stated they would be there for me and the child; they also explained that because of their religious beliefs they could not celebrate Christmas or birthdays (they sent gifts just before Christmas and birthdays every year until their deaths). At the time, I did not understand how much my life would change in a few months. As people realized I was pregnant, in high school and not hiding it anymore, I lost friends, was talked about, and became the subject of gossip. There is a saying that sticks and stones will break your bones, but words will never hurt you. That saying is a lie straight from the pit of hell. Words hurt!

I quickly realized not everyone would be supportive; however, I had two champions (my parents) and a village of people who provided guidance and encouragement in uncharted territory. Now, supportive did not mean my parents were going to take over raising my child and I would continue to be a teenager; they made that quite clear. The rules were set prior to me giving birth. Yet they were my parents and were going to make sure I was successful and finished high school and college. On the other hand, others had different opinions and were not afraid to tell me what they thought. I was told I was nothing, would not amount to anything and would end up on welfare. Well, I praise God daily that I did not listen to those malicious, hurtful words; instead, I used them to fuel my desire to overcome and succeed.

On October 24, 1983, I was in high school taking an Algebra test and I felt funny. The teacher must have seen me twist and turn in my chair because he stopped the class from taking the test, called the school nurse and had a student walk me to the office. The nurse immediately called my mom. My mom arrived at school and took me to the hospital. Once we arrived at the hospital, she called everyone to let them know the baby was on the way. One hour later, my daughter was born; she was beautiful, had a full head of hair and was premature by two months but was healthy. Once I was in the recovery room, the nurse came in and let me know I had family in the waiting room. To my surprise, both families were there. All I can remember is my grandmother saying, "Lord, that is the wrong baby, she is so tiny, white and has straight black hair."

Three days later, reality hit! I was a mother—what was I going to do? I was only sixteen and responsible for someone else. She was not a baby doll; I could not take her back to the toy store. She was my daughter; I was responsible for a life. Once reality hit, I had no choice but to rise above my circumstances.

After high school graduation, I went to work and college part-time. Three years later, on January 1, 1987, I delivered my son. I was engaged to his father; it was our plan to get married, raise our children as a blended family and be happy. We were both employed, young and knew we had a plan; however, we did not understand the level of commitment, trust, and difficulty in raising a blended family with three children.

Through the years, I wondered if some of those hateful words were right. I fought every day to overcome society's stigmatisms about being a teenage parent. At times, I worked two jobs, a full-time and part-time job, and went to college at night just to make sure my children did not go without, or feel like they were missing out on events or the latest trends and activities. It was not easy, but God! Over the years, I have learned several life lessons that were key:

Have Faith:

My faith in God and his plan for my life sustained me through some exceedingly difficult times. I specifically remember the day I walked to the altar, gave my life to Christ, and told Him I could not do this without Him. I was emotionally drained, physically tired, and asked Him for a better life.

I knew I wanted better for my children. All I remember after my prayer is a voice saying, "I got you." God has led, kept, protected, and blessed me and my family beyond what I asked when I took that walk over thirty years ago.

It takes a Village:

The African proverb states, "It takes a village to raise a child." I can attest that it is true; as a single young parent, I needed a village. As I grew and matured as a single parent, my children were very active in sports and church activities; my parents stood in the gap when I was working and could not make it to their activities, especially football games, karate class or 5th grade swim class (I think my father became the class dad for the swim class). While I was at class at night, my parents and sister would watch my children. Their babysitter was their godmother; she went above and beyond what babysitters do. I believe my children's babysitter was a Godsend to me and my parents. Years ago, she taught me how to budget and coupon shop to get the best deals for the children's diapers, clothes, and food.

My church family—yes, my church family—supported me. Both of my parents had a Christian background and grew up in church. Years before I became pregnant, my mother joined my father's family church. During my childhood, we went to church; however, it was not until I had my daughter that I really began to pay attention in church and understand God's plan. My church family embraced, supported, and encouraged me and my children. I am not saying everyone did; there were a few who shook their heads. But the positive truly outweighed the negative. It was there at the church, between two highways, where hearts are strangely warmed, that I can say I received a solid spiritual foundation that allowed me to accept God's plan for my life, knowing He would use me for His purpose. It was there I learned to love God's Word, teach Bible Study, preach, lead Women's ministry and became a certified lay speaker. It was there my children attended Sunday school, sang in the choir, became acolytes, took their first communion, were worship leaders and experienced a jail visit through the youth program.

It was because of the solid foundation, the support of two pastors (one would later become my godmother) and encouragement that I was able to teach, speak and lead women's ministries internationally. To this day, I smile when I remember my church village and thank God for their prayers and encouraging words.

Strive for Excellence and Take Care of one another:

Over the years, there were many things my parents taught my sister and me. Two are etched in my memory. First, strive for excellence. My mother was the disciplinarian and did not like mediocracy, especially when it came to education. She pushed my sister and me to strive for excellence in school, college, and our professional careers. She did the same with her grandchildren; below average grades were not accepted. My father was the mediator; he would always come to everyone's rescue and explain life lessons.

On almost a daily basis, my mother used to remind my sister and me that we only had each other and that we had to take care of one another. It was not easy at times, especially when we were young because we were always fighting. Yet during our darkest days, we took care of each other. We raised our children together, supported each other, made decisions that were best for the children and told them the same. From elementary school to the present day, our children take care of one another. They have been there for each other during school fights, difficult relationships, and life events. To this day, I tell my children and now grandchildren the same thing: "Take care of one another."

Children watch and learn:

As parents, we want to see our children succeed in life, knowing we will not always be there to guide and protect them. We have a duty to raise and prepare them for life events. As I found out, raising children when you are young and learning yourself affects the child. They witness your mistakes, watch your failures and wink at your successes. I remember my grandmother once told me, "Remember, your children are watching you." From that point on, I took my children into consideration in every decision. My life was no longer about me, but about them. I had the responsibility to ensure that I succeeded so they could learn how to measure success and surpass my achievements.

Children's Fathers or a Father figure are essential:

I did not marry either of my children's fathers; in fact, I have not seen or spoken to them in years. One of them chose to miss the joy of being a parent. No matter what type of relationship I had with my children's fathers, I did not speak badly about them in front of my children. After all, they were my children's father; a part of them. At some point, children understand actions speak louder than words; they are resilient and smart. They figure it out; at least my children did, and I did not have to say a word.

I genuinely believe children need their fathers or at least a father figure in their life that would give them a perspective that I could not as their mother. Raising a daughter and son was difficult as a single parent; therefore, I relied on my father to help. He stepped in to teach my son lessons from a man's perspective, how to physically do "stuff" that I had no idea how to do. I could only teach my son what a woman expected from a good man. I specifically remember one example that my father taught my son that resonates with me today. We were preparing to move out of my parents' house and I specifically heard my father tell my son that he was going to be the man of the house and it was his responsibility to make sure the house was secured every night. At thirteen, my son took that lesson to heart. Every night until he left for college, my son was the last to go to bed, made sure every door was locked, lights turned off, and most nights, removed my glasses, as I had a habit of falling asleep while reading in bed. That one lesson taught him accountability and how to protect his family.

My daughter needed a different relationship from a father figure. My dad was and still is her "go to" person. From the first time he held her, they have been close. Always the mediator, he would encourage her and be the sounding board between us. To this day, she will tell you, "That is my dad."

Each Child Is Different:

I had to learn my children were quite different. I could not communicate with or show love to them the same way. I had to learn that it was not about my communication style or about me, but about them. Life during their teenage years was not easy. One year, I experienced the most difficult and humbling experience as a parent: learning that my children had their own personalities, desires, and goals. I had an idea of how I wanted to mold and shape them and make sure they did not make the same mistakes I did. I remember it was three against one (I had my niece with me) and I had to call for backup; yes, I had to call my mother and she came for a three-week visit. While she was with us, she reminded me that I no longer had young children living with me, but teenagers, and I had to take the time to know the young man and woman who were living in my house; they were not children anymore and were learning their own style. I had raised them well and now it was time to change my parenting style to more leading and guiding than directing. Once my mother left, we still had some bumps in the road, but through a lot of prayer, guidance and support from my friends who became family while living abroad, we made it.

The Mom In Me

Everyone Needs a Champion:

In the beginning of my professional career, long ago, I was taught new employees needed at least three people: A Mentor, an Advisor, and a Champion. The Champion's responsibility is to speak on your behalf and be an advocate for you so when leadership opportunities arise, you are considered for the best positions; they put their name on the line for you.

I will say in life, everyone needs those three roles, especially children. Be your children's champion! Do not put your issues on them; instead, advocate for them and teach them to be the best adult they can be. As parents, we are our children's first mentor, advisor, and champion. We are responsible for their wellbeing, no matter how you became a parent.

I learned a long time ago that Champions have specific roles, from parents to babysitters who become godparents to your children to pastors who become your second mom to friends who have different perspectives but have been with you through your most difficult days.

Be your children's CHAMPION! Make sure they succeed! Support and love them because they are a gift!

To my known and unknown Champions, thank you; I could not have survived being sixteen and pregnant without your prayers and support.

To My Best Advocate and Champion:

It was not until I was at home with my mother, months before her death, that I realized how much she had given of her life to make sure her family was taken care of, loved and protected. She made unknown sacrifices that I will be forever grateful for. It is because of my mother's dedication, love, and sacrifice that I am the successful woman I am today. Without her encouragement, strong stance, faith, and trust in God and, yes,

228

sometimes, a good laying-out, I never would have made it through the difficult times. There were days where she would just tell me like it was and that was that. She taught me so many life lessons; there isn't a day that I don't miss my Mother. Mommy, *I love you more*!

My prayer:

My prayer for every young, single parent who thinks they cannot make it out of their circumstance is that you can! Let me encourage you to fight, pray, set goals, stay encouraged and look for mentors who have been where you are and have made it. We are here!

Remember, it is not where you start that counts but the legacy you leave that matters!

AFTERWORD

What could I have done differently, how did I miss the signs, am I really a horrible mother? These are just some of the questions I have pondered along my journey of motherhood. However, in my heart of hearts, I know I did the best that I could at the time. Now that my children are grown, there are a million things I wish I would have done differently. However, I must be at peace knowing that my efforts were to do right by them and not to harm them. I know that I am not alone. We will all have situations and circumstances that we ponder in hindsight.

With each stage of our children's lives we are left to figure it out, doing the best we can, given the state of mind that we are in. As I have stated before, there is no perfect mom on this earth. So, let's continue to extend grace to ourselves. For every wrong thing I think I have done as a mother my children let me know that I have done a ton of things right. Whether it be apologizing for letting a curse word slip in my presence, extending a hand to help me down the stairs, opening the car door for me, or refusing to let me walk on the outer part of a sidewalk, I know they love me and they know that I love them. In the end that's what really matters. Everything else is fixable.

I hope that you found encouragement, hope, helpful advice, and a sense of acceptance in this motherhood posse. We are all in this together.

Blessings,

Kimmoly K. LaBoo

ABOUT THE VISIONARY AUTHOR

Kimmoly K. LaBoo is a Published Author, International Speaker and Certified Master Life Coach. She is at the helm of LaBoo Publishing Enterprise, as CEO and founder. She is a highly respected change agent in her community and around the world.

Her award-winning company was created for the independent self-publisher. Kimmoly enjoys providing expert guidance and unlimited support to her clients, helping them recognize their brilliance, sharing their stories with the world, as writers.

She has dedicated her life to serving girls and women through mentoring, and coaching. Her compassionate coaching style, challenges clients to embrace change and show up confidently, using their unique gifts and talents to impact and serve others.

She was recently named among the Top 25 Women in Business by Courageous Woman magazine. She has appeared on Think Tech Hawaii, WPB Networks, Heaven 600, ABC2News, FOX5 News, and has graced many stages speaking and training to include, Department of Veterans Affairs, Blacks in Government National Training Conference, and Coppin State University.

Kimmoly is the mother of two amazing sons and currently resides in Baltimore, Maryland.

Contact Information:
www.laboopublishing.com
staff@laboopubishing.com

ALSO BY KIMMOLY K. LABOO

Set Apart and Chosen
God uses ordinary women to do extraordinary things

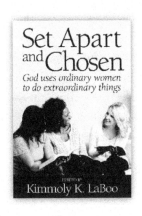

God never reveals His entire plan for our lives. If He did, we would likely be overwhelmed and immediately abort the plan out of fear. Instead, He carefully weaves His plans and our choices together for good. Set Apart and Chosen, God uses ordinary women to do extraordinary things is the intricate look into the lives of twenty extraordinary women who have overcome great odds to walk fully in the gift God has given them. It is said that hindsight is 20/20. We invite you into our lives in hopes that you will gain strength, clarity, courage, and boldness, to step out on faith, claiming everything that God has purposed for your life. The women in this book have discovered, even though they didn't understand their trials while amidst them, God has now given them great revelation about their gifts and how they are to use what they have overcome to bless the lives of others. Maybe you are in a season of your life where you can't see your way forward. We invite you to share in our victories, realizing God shows no partiality. If He was gracious enough to see us through, He can and will do it for you.

Paperback, 204 pages, ISBN 978-1732810457

A Threefold Cord Broken
What happens when Christian marriages fail

A Threefold Cord Broken is an honest, heartfelt depiction of the journey seven courageous Christian women experienced during the challenge of divorce. Each gives a glimpse into their marriage, what went wrong, how they navigated the process as a Christian, how they overcame, the lessons learned, and where they are now. The stories shared will give insight, hope, courage, and healing to others. It will enlighten those who think God has abandoned them or will somehow continually punish them for their choice to divorce. Encouraging, confirming, and reminding women that God may hate divorce, but He will never hate them. A valuable resource for those who are engaged, married, separated, or divorced.

Paperback, 78 pages, ISBN 978-1981529605

The Black Father Perspective
What we want America to know

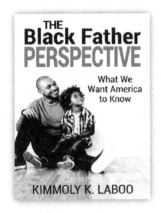

Black fathers play a pivotal role in the lives of our black children. According to the 2011 U.S. Census, nearly 2 in 3 (64%) African American children live in father-absent homes. However, we know all fathers are not absent. Society would have us to believe that black fathers are either in jail, or on drugs and are no good to the community. The Black Father Perspective is a collaboration of men who have come together to give voice to a population that is often overlooked and underappreciated. It is time to change the narrative. It is time to shift the agenda. Ten black fathers share their view on legacy, marriage, divorce, single parenting, teenage parenting, incarceration, child support and so much more. Reading this book will give you a new perspective of Black Fathers in America. This is what they want you to know.

Paperback, 140 pages, ISBN 978-1735112602

Made in USA - Kendallville, IN
1182825_9781735112664
10.23.2020 1625